COPS, CAMERAS, AND CRISIS

Cops, Cameras, and Crisis

The Potential and the Perils of
Police Body-Worn Cameras

Michael D. White and Aili Malm

NEW YORK UNIVERSITY PRESS
New York

NEW YORK UNIVERSITY PRESS
New York
www.nyupress.org

References to Internet websites (URLs) were accurate at the time of writing. Neither the author nor New York University Press is responsible for URLs that may have expired or changed since the manuscript was prepared.

ISBN: 978-1-4798-7453-8 (hardback)
ISBN: 978-1-4798-0328-6 (paperback)

For Library of Congress Cataloging-in-Publication data, please contact the Library of Congress.

New York University Press books are printed on acid-free paper, and their binding materials are chosen for strength and durability. We strive to use environmentally responsible suppliers and materials to the greatest extent possible in publishing our books.

Manufactured in the United States of America

10 9 8 7 6 5 4 3 2 1

Also available as an ebook

For our kids

CONTENTS

ACKNOWLEDGMENTS

Our thoughts on police body-worn cameras have been shaped by our colleagues, and we owe a debt of gratitude for their wisdom and experience. We are especially grateful to Barak Ariel, Anthony Braga, James "Chip" Coldren, Scott Decker, Hank Fradella, Janne Gaub, Chuck Katz, Daniel Lawrence, John Markovic, Dina Perrone, Denise Rodriguez, Craig Uchida, Jerry Ratcliffe, Shellie Solomon, Bill Sousa, Charles Stephenson, Natalie Todak, Craig Uchida, and Tom Woodmansee. We also are very thankful for the dozen or so police and criminal justice leaders who contributed their own personal observations in the book: Arif Alikhan, Kathy Armstrong, Brenda Buren, Edward A. Flynn, Gary Jenkins, Michael J. Kurtenbach, Steve Marcin, Damon Mosler, Carolyn Naoroz, Paul M. Noel, Geoffrey D. Smith, Seth Stoughton, and Dan Zehnder. These practitioner perspectives are the most valuable part of the book, and we are indebted to them for their contributions. We also thank Ilene Kalish and the staff at NYU Press.

1

Setting the Stage

Innovation, the Current Crisis, and Police Body-Worn Cameras

When you put a camera on a police officer, they tend to behave a little better, follow the rules a little better, . . . and if a
citizen knows the officer is wearing a camera, chances are
the citizen will behave a little better.
—William A. Farrar, Chief of Police, Rialto (California)
Police Department (Lovett, "In California")

We are unable to detect any statistically significant effects.
As such, our experiment suggests that we should recalibrate
our expectations of BWCs. Law enforcement agencies (particularly in contexts similar to Washington, DC) that are
considering adopting BWCs should not expect dramatic reductions in use of force or complaints, or other large-scale
shifts in police behavior, solely from the deployment of this
technology.
—Yokum, Ravishankar, and Coppock, *Evaluating the Effects
of Police Body-Worn Cameras*

Over the past 150 years, technological innovation has redefined the
very nature of policing, from the development of the call box in the
late 1800s to automobile patrol, the two-way radio, and 911 systems in
the twentieth century.[1] Technology has continued to reshape policing
into the twenty-first century, and the past forty years have arguably
been the most innovative in the history of the profession. In terms
of strategies, the emergence of problem-oriented policing (POP) and

community-oriented policing (COP) laid a foundation for a host of new strategies including hot spots policing, focused deterrence, intelligence-led policing, and predictive policing.[2] These innovations have been complemented by the development of new tools such as geographic information systems (GIS), crime analysis, CompStat, DNA and forensics, license plate readers, less lethal alternatives (TASER), drug and alcohol field testing, and gunshot detection systems.

The tremendous innovation in how police go about their daily business (strategies) and the tools they use to conduct that business (technologies) has been increasingly grounded in evidence-based policing. Police leadership organizations, researchers, and practitioners have worked to build a body of knowledge that applies rigorous research methodologies to the study of innovation in policing, both tools and strategies, and that charts a course forward into the twenty-first century. There are now multiple directories of evidence-based police strategies and tools, such as CrimeSolutions.gov and George Mason University's Evidence-Based Policing Matrix.[3] And there are police-led organizations devoted entirely to the diffusion of evidence-based practice in the United States and abroad.[4] For example, after the second annual conference of the American Society of Evidence-Based Policing, *BBC News* published a story about the organization and the "pracademics" (working police officers who conduct research in their organizations) who are advancing the principles of data- and research-driven decision-making.[5] Evidence-based policing provides an important lens for examining the diffusion and impact of innovations in policing. So it should come as no surprise that we use this lens to study police body-worn cameras.

Cameras in Policing

The past few decades have also been defined by an increasing reliance on technology as a mechanism for surveillance, both by citizens and by the police. In the early 1990s, dashboard cameras emerged as a method for capturing the real-time encounters between police and citizens. Despite early resistance to dashboard cameras by officers,[6] research demonstrated that the cameras led to increased officer safety and accountability and reduced agency liability.[7] As a result, the technology has been widely embraced by law enforcement. A survey by the Bureau of Justice Statistics in 2013 indicated that 68 percent of responding agencies had deployed in-car camera systems.[8] Closed circuit surveillance systems (CCTV) have also become increasingly popular among police both as a method of surveillance (crime prevention) and as a tool for post hoc criminal investigation (e.g., the Boston Marathon bombing).[9] The proliferation of smartphones has also exponentially increased the ability to record events as they transpire, especially police-citizen encounters.[10] As a result, cameras have become a ubiquitous part of life in the twenty-first century.[11]

The most recent surveillance technology for policing is officer body-worn cameras (BWCs). Sander Flight states, "Bodycams are small cameras that are worn on the person, that have at least one microphone and an internal data storage that allows audio and video footage to be recorded."[12] Law enforcement interest in BWCs can be traced back to the early 2000s, when several police departments in the United Kingdom began experimenting with the technology.[13] Interest in the United States grew slowly throughout the first decade of the twenty-first century, as a handful of police departments deployed BWCs (e.g., Oakland and Albuquerque).[14] The technology gained significant attention in August 2013, when Judge Shira Scheindlin, of the federal district court in Manhattan, ruled that the stop, question, and frisk (SQF) program of the New York Police Department (NYPD) was unconstitutional and ordered officers in the highest volume SQF precincts to wear BWCs in an effort to prevent racial profiling (see Box 1.1).[15] One month later, the Police Executive Research Forum (PERF) held a one-day conference on police BWCs, which led to a published report in early 2014.[16] At approximately the same time, the Diagnostic Center of the US Department of Justice contracted with one of us to write an "Assessing the Evidence" report on police BWCs.[17] In 2013, the Bureau of Justice Statistics added BWC questions to its Law Enforcement Management and Administrative Statistics

(LEMAS) survey, and Brian Reaves noted that "an estimated 32% (about 3,900) of departments reported they provided body-worn cameras for at least some of their patrol officers."[18] In short, BWCs had already begun to garner attention among law enforcement before the summer of 2014. In July and August 2014, the dialogue surrounding policing and BWCs in the United States changed dramatically.

BOX 1.1

"Because body-worn cameras are uniquely suited to addressing the constitutional harms at issue in this case, I am ordering the NYPD to institute a pilot project in which body-worn cameras will be worn for a one-year period by officers on patrol in one precinct per borough— specifically the precinct with the highest number of stops during 2012. The Monitor will establish procedures for the review of stop recordings by supervisors and, as appropriate, more senior managers. The Monitor will also establish procedures for the preservation of stop recordings for use in verifying complaints in a manner that protects the privacy of those stopped. Finally, the Monitor will establish procedures for measuring the effectiveness of body-worn cameras in reducing unconstitutional stops and frisks."
—Judge Shira Scheindlin, August 12, 2013 (remedies order in *Floyd et al. v. City of New York*, 959 F. Supp. 2d 540 (2013), www.nysd .uscourts.gov)

Summer 2014: The Crisis in Policing Emerges

On July 17, 2014, NYPD officers approached Eric Garner on a street corner in Staten Island because they suspected he was selling unlicensed cigarettes. Officers attempted to take Garner into custody, and during the struggle, police officer Daniel Pantaleo applied a choke hold. Garner stated nearly a dozen times that he could not breathe. Garner lost consciousness after the struggle, and he was pronounced dead an hour later. The entire incident was captured on a bystander's cell phone.

On August 9, 2014, Ferguson police officer Darren Wilson stopped Michael Brown and Dorian Johnson. Though there is no video of the incident and the facts are disputed, it is clear the initial stop led to a struggle between Wilson, who was still seated in his patrol car, and Brown. Officer Wilson fired one shot while he was still in his car and then several more shots after he exited the vehicle, killing Brown. Protests and civil disorder began within hours of Brown's death and continued for several days. On August 16, Governor Jay Nixon of Missouri declared a state of emergency in Ferguson. On November 24, a grand jury declined to indict Officer Wilson for Michael Brown's death, and riots again exploded on the streets of Ferguson. Controversial police killings of minority citizens continued over the next few years: Tamir Rice in Cleveland, Walter Scott in North Charleston, Freddie Gray in Baltimore, Samuel DuBose in Cincinnati, Laquan McDonald in Chicago, Alton Sterling in Baton Rouge, Philando Castile near St. Paul, Justine Damond in Minneapolis. Public outrage over these (and other) incidents produced civil disorder in several cities, created strong antipolice sentiment, and led to a national movement demanding police reform (i.e., Black Lives Matter: http://blacklivesmatter.com).

The White House responded quickly to the crisis in policing. Within four months of Michael Brown's death in Ferguson, former president Barack Obama announced several initiatives to address the emerging crisis, and police body-worn cameras (BWCs) were central to the federal response. In December 2014, President Obama debuted a plan to strengthen community policing through enhanced police training, equipment, and review of policy (figure 1.1).[19] Police BWCs were a critical piece of the community policing plan. In fact, President Obama pledged $75 million for the deployment of more than fifty thousand BWCs (see Box 1.2).[20] The president also announced the creation of the President's Task Force on 21st Century Policing, and he "charged the task force with identifying best practices and offering recommendations" to build community trust and enhance police accountability.[21] The President's Task Force, which held "listening sessions" across the country and

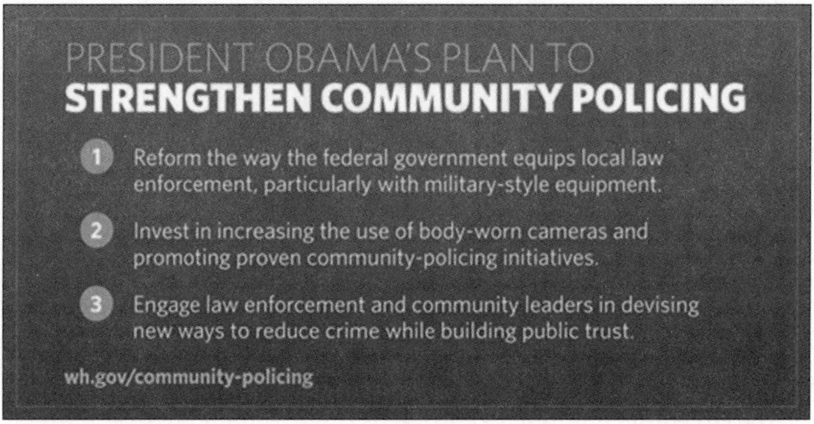

FIGURE 1.1. President Obama's community policing plan

heard testimony from police leaders, researchers, civil rights advocates, and citizens, issued its final report in 2015. The final report includes more than sixty recommendations for change, and BWCs are highlighted as a tool that may enhance citizens' trust in police and improve police accountability. In plain terms, BWCs quickly became part of the equation for improving policing in the United States (see Box 1.3).

BOX 1.2

"I am going to be proposing some new community policing initiatives that will significantly expand funding and training for local law enforcement, including up to 50,000 additional body-worn cameras for law enforcement agencies."
—President Barack Obama, December 1, 2014 (Reuters, "Obama Calls for Body Cameras on Police")

BOX 1.3

"Despite the fact that Milwaukee had consistent declines in police use of force and citizen complaints, tensions remain among some

> residents and the police department. Those tensions are exacerbated by critical incidents in the city and news coverage of critical police incidents in other cities. In response to this, body-worn cameras have the potential to enhance community trust through increased transparency and accountability."
> —Edward A. Flynn, Chief (retired), Milwaukee Police Department (authors' interview)

Police BWCs diffused rapidly in US policing after the summer of 2014. The Major Cities Chiefs and Major County Sheriffs conducted a survey of its membership in 2015 and estimated that all large police agencies would have BWC programs in the next few years.[22] PERF conducted a national survey of law enforcement agencies in 2015 and found that "more than 35% of respondents indicated that their agencies currently use BWCs, and almost 47% of respondents said they have plans to deploy cameras in the future. So more than eight out of 10 agencies either were using BWCs or were planning to do so."[23] The Bureau of Justice Statistics (BJS) added BWC questions to its 2016 LEMAS survey. The results, published in November 2018, show that 47 percent of all law enforcement agencies have deployed BWCs, including 80 percent of large agencies (five hundred or more sworn officers).[24]

The rapid adoption of BWCs is explained by several factors. First, BWCs are supported across a diverse range of sectors that are often at odds with each other, including police leadership organizations (International Association of Chiefs of Police [IACP]),[25] civil rights groups (American Civil Liberties Union [ACLU]),[26] police unions,[27] and citizens.[28] Though all of the stakeholders have their own, often competing ideas about the goals, form, and function of a BWC program, there has been near universal support for the technology in principle. Second, since 2015 the US Department of Justice (DOJ) has awarded nearly $60 million in grants to more than 330 law enforcement agencies, resulting in the deployment of more than seventy thousand BWCs across the country (i.e., a realization of former president Obama's December 2014 pledge).[29]

Third, DOJ has made available a wide range of resources to facilitate the adoption of BWCs, such as a National Body-Worn Camera Toolkit,[30] a training and technical assistance mechanism,[31] and tools such as a Law Enforcement Implementation Checklist and a BWC Policy Review Scorecard.[32] Last, the rapid diffusion of police BWCs has also been driven by findings from several early research studies that suggested the technology can generate a wide range of positive effects for police, citizens, and the relationship between the two.

The Evidence Base on Police BWCs

The purported benefits of BWCs go directly to the core mission of the police. Advocates claim BWCs can lead to increased transparency and accountability, improved police legitimacy, officer support, reductions in use of force and complaints against officers (both citizen and internal), and enhanced quality of evidence (leading to improved prosecutorial and court outcomes) and can facilitate effective training (see table 1.1). PERF's recent national survey collected information on reasons for BWC adoption, and more than 90 percent of agencies indicated they deployed BWCs "to promote accountability, transparency, and legitimacy."[33]

TABLE 1.1. Benefits and Concerns of Body-Worn Cameras

Benefits	Concerns
• Transparency	• Privacy concerns
• Accountability	• Officer safety
• Officer support	• Management of public expectations
• Citizen support/legitimacy	• Officer/union buy-in
• Reductions in use of force and complaints (citizen and internal)	• Impact on officer activity (depolicing)
	• Impact on officer discretion
• Evidentiary benefits (enhanced prosecutor and court outcomes)	• Financial and resource commitment
• Training capacities	

Alternatively, critics have identified a number of concerns with BWCs, such as potential violations of citizens' and officers' privacy, threats to officers' safety, unreasonable public expectations, officers' resistance to the technology, reductions in officers' proactivity, negative impact on officers' discretion, and an enormous financial and resource commitment required for such an expensive, labor-intensive undertaking.

Research has informed the debate over BWCs. In 2014, for example, Michael White noted that most of the claims about BWCs were untested, and he identified fewer than five rigorous, empirical studies of the technology.[34] Less than two years later, Cynthia Lum and colleagues identified more than fifty published or ongoing studies examining the impact of police BWCs on a range of outcomes.[35] In 2019, Lum et al. published a comprehensive narrative review of seventy empirical BWC studies.[36] Several early studies of BWCs suggested the technology could produce positive outcomes, most notably reductions in use of force and citizen complaints. The first and most widely publicized study examined BWCs in Rialto (California). The Rialto study, published in 2013, was carried out by former chief Tony Farrar as part of his graduate study at Cambridge University. The project, a randomized controlled trial, documented year-to-year reductions of nearly 90 percent in citizen complaints and 60 percent in use of force, following deployment of BWCs (see Farrar's quote at the beginning of this chapter).[37] As the crisis in policing emerged in the summer of 2014, advocates of the technology pointed to the Rialto study as evidence that BWCs could be a potential "silver bullet" that would address the problems between police and minority communities.

The case for BWCs grew quickly as similarly positive results were reported in other early studies of BWCs in Mesa (Arizona),[38] Phoenix (Arizona),[39] and Orlando (Florida).[40] More recent BWC studies have also reported substantial reductions in force and citizen complaints: Spokane (Washington),[41] Tampa (Florida),[42] Las Vegas (Nevada),[43] and the United Kingdom.[44] Notably, many of these studies were randomized controlled trials (RCTs; Las Vegas, Orlando, Rialto, Spokane) or used strong quasi-experimental designs (Mesa, Phoenix, Tampa, United Kingdom).

Several studies have also highlighted the evidentiary value of BWCs, particularly for domestic violence cases.[45] White and colleagues found a connection between awareness of a BWC and enhanced perceptions of procedural justice.[46] Also, several studies have demonstrated high levels of both officer and citizen support for BWCs.[47] Anthony Braga and colleagues conducted the first robust cost-benefit analysis of BWCs, and they found that the technology generated savings of more than $4 million per year in Las Vegas.[48] These quickly mounting positive research findings undoubtedly contributed to the rapid adoption of BWCs in law enforcement, both in the United States and abroad.

However, a number of more recent research studies have not found positive effects. Several studies documented no impact on use of force, citizen complaints, or both.[49] The quote from Yokum and colleagues at the beginning of the chapter highlights their conclusion that BWCs did not affect use of force or citizen complaints in Washington, DC.[50] Barak Ariel and colleagues reported a troubling association between BWCs and increased rates of assaults on officers.[51] Both of these studies were RCTs. There has also been strong resistance to BWCs in some jurisdictions. In August 2016, the Boston police union sought an injunction in federal court to stop the department leadership from creating a BWC program.[52] A recent series of police killings of citizens that were not captured by the officers' BWCs has caused public outrage about officers' failure to activate their cameras (e.g., the case of Justine Damond).[53] Citizens in Sacramento protested when BWC footage indicated that officers muted their cameras in the immediate aftermath of shooting Stephon Clark.[54]

Some critics view BWCs as part of a larger movement to publicly scrutinize police and have argued that cameras may lead officers to engage in depolicing.[55] Braga et al. concluded that the benefits of BWCs with regard to force and complaint reductions may be offset by increases in formal activity, especially in minority communities: "Alternatively, increased enforcement activity could undermine police legitimacy if citizens view heightened arrests and citations as harmful to their communities."[56] Taken together, the mixed findings have led many people to question the value of adopting police BWCs (see Box 1.4).

BOX 1.4

Recent Media Headlines about BWCs

"The Failure of Police Body Cameras"
—Lopez, *Vox*, July 21, 2017

"Police Body Cameras: Money for Nothing?"
—*Fox News*, October 20, 2017

"Body Cameras Have Little Effect on Police Behavior, Study Says"
—Ripley and Williams, *New York Times*, October 20, 2017

"Body Cameras Aren't Working. So What's Next?"
—Ikem and Ogbeifun, *Huffington Post*, November 28, 2017

"Scorecard of 50 Local Police Body Camera Programs Shows Nationwide Failure to Protect Civil Rights and Privacy"
—Inouye, Leadership Conference, August 2, 2016

The Focus of Cops, Cameras, and Crisis

The rapidly growing and increasingly mixed body of research on police BWCs poses two problems for police practitioners and researchers. First, it is difficult to keep track of the quickly growing evidence base. New studies seem to become available almost weekly. Some research, like the Washington, DC, study or the Las Vegas study, draws national media attention. Other research studies are published in academic journals with restricted access and receive no attention at all. And other studies, particularly internal reports by law enforcement agencies, may not be released publicly. Staying on top of the latest in BWC-related research is no easy task! In fact, by the time this book goes to print, there will no doubt be some new BWC studies.

Second, it is difficult to make sense of the sometimes competing findings across studies. The two quotes at the beginning of this chapter illustrate this point. The first quote, from former chief Farrar, describes the BWC experience in Rialto (California). The deployment of BWCs in Rialto was followed by extraordinary year-to-year reductions in officer use force and citizen complaints, and a recent follow-up study showed that those findings have persisted over time.[57] Alternatively, the Washington, DC, study found no impact at all on the same two outcomes. How can this be? How can deployment of BWCs in two jurisdictions produce findings that are so different? And perhaps more importantly, what does the increasingly mixed body of research evidence mean for the continued adoption of police BWCs?

This is where *Cops, Cameras, and Crisis* comes in. This book is intended to serve as a go-to resource for those who are interested in police body-worn cameras. The bulk of the book delves deeply into the claims made about BWCs by both advocates and critics, coupled with an exhaustive examination of the research base on each of those claims. Chapter 2 is devoted to the perceived benefits of BWCs, and chapter 3 addresses the challenges and limitations of the technology. For each perceived benefit (enhanced transparency and legitimacy, accountability, reductions in force and complaints, evidentiary value, etc.) and each perceived concern (privacy, officer safety, officer proactivity, cost, etc.), we concisely review the evidence and offer assessments of the veracity of the claims. Based on the weight of the evidence, what can we conclude about the impact of BWCs on police legitimacy? What can we conclude about the impact of BWCs on use of force? What can we conclude about the impact of BWCs on officer safety? What can we conclude about the impact of BWCs on officer proactivity? In chapters 2 and 3, we answer these questions. Moreover, throughout the book we use quotes and vignettes from experts in the field who have hands-on experience with police BWCs to illustrate important points and to bolster our conclusions.

In chapters 2 and 3, we also offer insights on the potential reasons for variation in research findings. Three issues, in particular, are highlighted. First, police departments that deploy BWCs often have very different "starting points." Some departments, like Rialto,[58] Ferguson, or the NYPD, implement BWCs in the wake of a scandal. An agency that adopts BWCs following a misconduct scandal has a very different starting point than does an agency that adopts BWCs as part of a continued professionalization effort or after years of federal oversight (like the Washington, DC, Metropolitan Police Department). The bottom line is that the "state" of an agency predeployment will affect the implementation and impact of a BWC program.

The second issue we highlight is program planning and implementation. The deployment of BWCs is a highly complex undertaking that touches nearly every aspect of police operations. The costs, financial and otherwise, are substantial. However, the current political environment in many jurisdictions emphasizes rapid deployment of BWCs, often at the expense of proper planning.[59] The Ferguson (Missouri) Police Department, for example, deployed BWCs within one month of Michael Brown's death.[60] The consequences of poor BWC program planning are significant, from resistance among line officers to low or no usage by downstream criminal justice actors (e.g., prosecutors) and backlash from citizens. In plain terms, the costs of BWCs are high; the level of difficulty is high; the stakes are high; and the benefits are by no means guaranteed. Proper planning and implementation is critically important.

The third issue that can explain mixed findings involves the research itself. Not all research is created equal, and a handful of research-method-related questions can dramatically alter the likelihood of documenting positive effects. How were officers selected to receive BWCs? Was the selection process random, or did the department solicit volunteers? Does the study include a non-BWC group as a comparison? How did the researchers measure their outcomes? If the study was a randomized controlled trial, did the researchers randomize officers to BWC and non-BWC groups, or did they randomize shifts? Did the authors account for the degree to which BWC and non-BWC officers interact? All of these questions address points that affect the outcomes of a BWC study and, at least in part, explain the mixed research findings.

In chapter 4, we examine the past, present, and future of police BWCs through two different, complementary lenses. The first is the diffusion of innovations framework. Diffusion of innovation refers to the spread of an idea, information, tool, or practice from a source to a larger group.[61] Whether an innovation spreads, as well as the rate of diffusion, is greatly affected by a number of things. Barbara Wejnert developed a conceptual framework that includes three different sets of factors that can influence diffusion: characteristics of the innovation (public and private consequences, costs and benefits), the innovators (nature of the entity, status, and personal characteristics) and the environment (geographical and political conditions and societal culture).[62] We apply this framework to explore the adoption of police BWCs to date and assess the prospects for continued diffusion in the future.

The second lens is the evidence-based policing framework. Carl Sagan masterfully stated, "A central lesson of science is that to understand complex issues (or even simple ones), we must try to free our minds of dogma and to guarantee the freedom . . . to experiment. Arguments from authority are unacceptable."[63] This is the essence of evidence-based policing—using science to advance the field from one based almost exclusively on authority to one rooted in science. According to the United Kingdom College of Policing's definition, "in an evidence-based policing approach, police officers and staff create, review and use the best available evidence to inform and challenge policies, practices and decisions."[64] Because BWCs can impact policing in so many ways and the body of research has grown so quickly, it is important to critically evaluate the evidence for the practitioner audience. In this book, we apply this approach to assess the evidence base for BWCs and offer guidance to police leadership. Both the diffusion of innovation and evidence-based policing frameworks provide insights on the how and why questions regarding current rates of BWC adoption, and just as important, they provide an informed position to consider the prospects for BWCs in the future.

The application of these two frameworks sets the stage for the fifth and final chapter of *Cops, Cameras, and Crisis*. We have two objectives in chapter 5. The first is a forward-looking review of the next set of challenges for BWC adopters. These challenges span the factors that can influence diffusion (characteristics of the innovation, innovators, and environment) and center on both human and technological elements of a BWC program. We assess the next set of human-based challenges with BWCs, such as addressing activation compliance (and dealing with low-end activators), addressing controversies surrounding the public release of video and officers' authority to review video after a critical incident (e.g., a shooting), managing citizen and other nonuser expectations of the technology (handling the onset of a "CSI effect" with BWCs, where if there is no video, then it did not happen), and being responsive to changing laws on evidence, privacy, and access to BWC footage. We also consider emerging technological innovations such as automatic activation, the integration of BWCs and facial recognition, and the role and use of "big data" with BWCs.

The second objective centers on planning and implementation. More specifically, we delve into how law enforcement agencies can navigate the well-known and newly emerging challenges surrounding BWCs in order to increase the likelihood of achieving positive outcomes. In particular, we focus on a "best-practice" implementation guide developed by the US Department of Justice, called the "Law Enforcement Implementation Checklist." The Checklist, which is grounded in the evidence base on effective program implementation in criminal justice settings,[65] provides over two dozen steps for an agency to follow and centers on six core principles: learn the fundamentals; develop a plan; form a working group; develop policy; define the technology solution (procurement); communicate with and educate stakeholders; and execute phased rollout/implementation. We argue that adherence to the best-practices guide will lead to successful BWC implementation, will generate high levels of integration and acceptance among a variety of stakeholders inside and outside the police department, and ultimately, will lead to achievement of positive outcomes.

Cops, Cameras, and Crisis concludes with a few important takeaway messages. The first is that BWCs are here to stay. From both the diffusion of innovation and evidence-based policing frameworks, it is clear that BWCs will become a permanent part of the policing landscape in the United States and abroad. Diffusion will continue as new agencies adopt BWCs and current adopters expand use of the technology in the daily routine of their officers. Second, BWCs are a tool. They are not a "silver bullet" that can repair decades of mistrust between police and citizens. Nor can BWCs single-handedly put an end to bad policing. Expectations about the impact of BWCs should be realistic. Third, the evidence base on the impact of BWCs is remarkably robust in several key areas. The research is notable with regard to the consistency of findings, the speed at which the results have been produced, and the methodological rigor of the studies that have generated the evidence.

Fourth, the research base will continue to be mixed. The mixed findings are tied to a number of factors highlighted earlier and explored in depth in the forthcoming pages (e.g., the complexity of issues involved, the "state" of a police department pre-BWC deployment). There are nearly eighteen thousand law enforcement agencies in the United States. While there will not be eighteen thousand different BWC stories, there will certainly be more than one, and in fact, there may be many. Last, we conclude that the benefits of BWCs can far outweigh the costs—if a BWC program is properly planned, implemented, and managed. As stated previously, the costs are high, the stakes are high, and the degree of difficulty is high. BWCs are not easy. They require a long-term, deep commitment by a law enforcement agency. But as we will show in this book, the commitment can pay important dividends on a range of critically important outcomes that help police achieve their core mission.

2

Are Body-Worn Cameras a "Silver Bullet" Solution?

Research on the Benefits of the Technology

There is no silver bullet. There are always options and the
options have consequences.
—Ben Horowitz, *The Hard Thing about Hard Things*

Much like the Taser and dashboard cameras in recent years, BWCs have
been touted as a "silver bullet" for the current crisis between police and
minority communities. Supporters of BWCs claim they lead to increased
trust in police, reductions in use of force and citizen complaints against
officers, increased quality of evidence, and enhanced training opportunities. But like past supposed cure-alls, the growing body of evidence
has shown that while BWCs certainly have benefits, they also have limits
and consequences.

In this chapter, we provide an overview of BWC evidence to assess the
benefits of the technology. We take a different approach from existing
reviews of BWC evidence.[1] Rather than organizing the evidence by an
article's central research question, we specifically examine reported benefits and limitations of the technology. For instance, we do not present
a thorough review of all citizen and officer perception research; this has
been done several times before. Instead, we explore the more pertinent
questions of police transparency, accountability, and legitimacy—all of
which are publicized as benefits of BWCs.

It will quickly become clear that some topics have received more attention than others. Use of force and complaints against police have
eclipsed other areas of BWC research. However, this does not mean
these outcomes are more important or serve as a singular proxy for

BWC success. It often simply means they are easier to operationalize and measure. So when discussing BWC benefits—building trust, the "civilizing effect," evidentiary value, and training benefits—we will not only review what we know but highlight what we do not.

We use graphical tables to illustrate research findings. We are also strong believers that a book like this needs practitioners' voices. We have been lucky to work with some officers and criminal justice professionals who have firsthand experience with BWCs. You will read some of their perspectives in the short vignettes throughout the next two chapters. These have been integrated with the academic research to bring a combination of evidence-based and practitioner-led insights on BWCs.

Building Trust in Police with BWCs: Transparency, Accountability, and Legitimacy

Trust between police and the communities they serve is critical. Police need citizens to cooperate and provide information about crimes, and communities need to believe that police respect community values. Trust is often identified as one of the core elements of police legitimacy, which Tom Tyler has defined as a "psychological property of an authority, institution, or social arrangement that leads those connected to it to believe that it is appropriate, proper, and just."[2] When citizens view the police as legitimate, they defer to authority through self-regulation, as people obey the police because they believe it is the right thing to do.[3] The real value of police legitimacy lies in the outcomes it can produce, most notably enhanced citizen compliance with police commands during an encounter, greater cooperation with police (reporting crimes, providing information about crimes, etc.), and obedience to the law.[4]

Though there are several mechanisms for generating police legitimacy, procedural justice has received the most scholarly attention. Procedural justice refers to the way in which police treat citizens and the fairness of the decisions that police make.[5] Prior research has identified four key components of procedural justice: citizen participation (being given the opportunity to state one's case), fairness and neutrality, dignity and respect, and trustworthy motives.[6] A large body of research has consistently demonstrated that procedurally just treatment of citizens can lead to improve views of police legitimacy.[7]

The current crisis in policing has eroded police legitimacy (and trust) in many communities, and BWCs have been identified as a potential alternative way to fix the problem. Most police departments adopt BWCs as a way to increase trust through improved transparency, accountability, and legitimacy,[8] but do they actually achieve their goal? Perceived success in each of these concepts might be different depending on whether you are speaking to the police, researchers, or the public. In this section, we explore each component in turn.

Transparency

Transparency is about being open and honest in communications and operations. For maximum transparency, BWC footage needs to be accessible to the public. But issues of cost, lack of redaction software, and privacy make complete transparency incredibly difficult. Police departments need to decide how transparent they want to be, especially surrounding critical incidents, and set up policies that carefully balance the costs and benefits. Some departments seek to increase transparency by implementing BWCs but actually decrease transparency by implementing policies that resist releasing camera footage to the public. Other departments more firmly commit to transparency by allowing fairly open access to police videos, especially for critical incidents. The Spokane Police Department, for example, created a citizens committee responsible for reviewing critical incident videos (see Box 2.1). In a community with some inherent trust in its police department, this might pass muster as being "transparent." Conversely, citizens in communities with low reserves of trust in police might apply a much more stringent definition of transparency and feel that nothing less than unfettered public access to video will suffice.

BOX 2.1

"Body-worn cameras allow community members to 'see' what happened during an incident rather than to hear about it secondhand. The Spokane Police Department engages Police Advisory Committee (PAC) members to review officer-involved shooting video prior to media release. Several PAC members have reported that the ability to review body-worn camera video is one of the most rewarding parts of volunteering with PAC. After viewing video footage, community members have a better understanding of the event, but they also have more questions, resulting in productive discussions with SPD [Spokane Police Department] leadership. Body-worn camera footage is invaluable for many reasons, but certainly the documentation of critical incidents is crucial to strengthening police accountability. PAC's review of videos from officer-involved shootings has led to a new level of enhanced transparency for the Spokane Police Department."

—Kathy Armstrong, Program Professional, Spokane Police Department (authors' interview)

Despite researchers in several jurisdictions documenting transparency as an indicator of BWC success, actual measurable improvement in transparency has been lacking. Research has come from two separate sources: citizen and officer perception studies. By and large, officer surveys and focus groups reveal that most officers believe BWCs would improve community trust due, in part, to increased transparency. The Las Vegas Metropolitan Police Department conducted preimplementation officer focus groups, and transparency was identified as one of the key perceived benefits to the department's BWC program.[9] William Pelfry and Steven Keener also completed focus groups, but this time in a large university police department. Command staff stated that because transparency was a primary motivation for securing BWCs, they went beyond the minimum legislated notification requirements and used BWC footage to facilitate the speed and precision of the public notices.[10] The Mesa

(Arizona) Police Department conducted a quasi-experiment with fifty patrol officers who wore BWCs and fifty matched non-BWC officers.[11] Eighty percent of officers thought that BWCs would improve the accuracy of officer accounts, leading to increased transparency.[12] However, some research suggests that these positive perceptions might change after BWCs have been implemented. For example, as part of a partially randomized experiment with the Hallandale Beach (Florida) Police Department, researchers conducted officer surveys before and after BWC implementation and found dramatic shifts in opinion, with officers increasingly feeling that BWC use would not improve transparency and accountability.[13]

Like officers, citizens generally agree that BWCs will increase police transparency. Researchers in Las Vegas (Nevada) administered an online survey to a US sample of 599 adult residents.[14] Over 90 percent of respondents believed that BWCs would increase the transparency of police work, and 61 percent believed that citizens would have greater trust in police due to BWCs. The majority of citizen perception studies dealing with transparency have clouded the terminology in this area, couching it under the procedural justice umbrella; as a result, these will be discussed under the "Legitimacy" heading later in the chapter.

Before moving to accountability, it is also important to discuss something called the "transparency double standard." This double standard occurs when the message to the community is one of transparency but officers are excluded from the BWC planning process.[15] Police officers are more motivated when they believe they are supported by their organization.[16] If line officers have been excluded from the BWC planning process, they may perceive lower levels of organizational justice and be more likely to resist the technology.[17] Officers' perceived disconnect between internal and external transparency may reduce their accountability and therefore, reduce community trust.[18] It is clear, therefore, that while transparency is a laudable aim, operationalizing it remains a challenge.

Accountability

Accountability involves holding law enforcement agencies and individual officers responsible for achieving the basic goals of policing: "reducing crime and disorder, enhancing the quality of neighborhood life, and providing fair, respectful, and equal treatment for all people."[19] BWCs can increase police accountability by providing an internal management tool to monitor and ensure good behavior and to hold officers accountable for their misbehavior (see Box 2.2). And just like transparency, accountability has been held up as an indicator of BWC success. However, actual measurable improvement of accountability due to BWCs has been scarce.

BOX 2.2

"BWCs provide an opportunity to look at daily police operations at a level not previously possible unless you were standing right next to an officer. BWCs are by no means the only gauge of performance, but they certainly provide an unfiltered insight. Never before in the history of our profession have leaders at a level above operations been able to look at officer performance in such detail. A police chief or sheriff, regardless of the size of their department, can now walk into their office every morning, sit down at their desk, access their computer, and look at the performance of any officer in their department and at any point in time. How many are doing so? Are officers upholding their department values? What does the video tell us about the department's organizational culture? Are officers performing their duties as trained and within legal standards? How a department answers and reacts to these questions can be an indicator of their accountability to themselves and the community they serve.

A solid police sergeant who reviews an officer's footage, corrects negative behavior resulting in performance change, can possibly save that officer's career. The same is true at the department level. BWCs might possibly be the most important risk-management tool a department can have. BWCs, as part of a strong departmental risk-management

process, might just save the department the negative consequences of a preventable controversial incident. Departments that don't consider this possibility do so at their own risk."
—Dan Zehnder, Captain (retired), Las Vegas Metropolitan Police Department, and President, Principis Group (authors' interview)

Citizen perception studies reveal that citizens believe BWCs increase police accountability. As mentioned in the "Transparency" section, researchers in Las Vegas (Nevada) used an online survey to discover that 61 percent of people believed that citizens will have greater trust in police due to BWCs. This speaks directly to accountability. Matthew Crow and colleagues surveyed residents in two Florida counties and found that respondents who hold police accountable for crime in their area held less favorable views on police performance and more positive views on the benefits of BWCs.[20] On the basis of a comprehensive review of studies, Lum and colleagues concluded, "many study findings (as well as widespread media coverage) indicate that citizens have supported police agencies acquiring BWCs and have high expectations for them with regard to making the police more accountable and increasing citizen confidence in the police."[21]

Legitimacy

Legitimacy presents the same definitional and measurement issues as transparency and accountability. However, prior research and theoretical work in the area of procedural justice provides a foundation to define and measure police legitimacy.[22] Researchers have measured BWCs' effect on legitimacy using different methodologies: citizen and officer surveys and systematic social observation of police-citizen encounters.

We would expect the public to perceive police with BWCs as being more legitimate. A couple of studies by Scott Culhane and colleagues tested this assumption by presenting one group of people with details on a police shooting case and another group with the same details plus BWC footage. In the researchers' first study, subjects shown BWC footage for the case were significantly more likely to rate the shooting as lawful and justified.[23] These results reversed in a replication conducted post-Ferguson, with the BWC group giving the lowest ratings for justifiability.[24] These contradictory results emphasize how current events can affect public perception of police legitimacy.

Since the Culhane studies, researchers have tried to better operationalize legitimacy by grounding it in the theory of procedural justice. Essentially, procedural justice posits that citizens prefer police to treat them in a fair and thoughtful manner.[25] Procedural justice is measured through four distinct elements: participation, neutrality, dignity and respect, and trustworthy motives. Four studies have assessed the effectiveness of BWCs on aspects of procedural justice in police-citizen encounters (see table 2.1). Each entry in table 2.1 includes basic information about the study: the agency, the state, the researchers, the year of the publication, and the rigor of the study as determined by its rating on the Maryland Scale of Scientific Methods (SMS).[26] The SMS rates the internal validity of a study on a five-point scale with one being the weakest and five being

TABLE 2.1. Procedural Justice Research

Agency	Location	Authors	Year	Rigor	Finding	Sample size
Anaheim PD	California	McClure et al.	2017	☐☐☐☐☐	⊘	◇
Arlington PD	Texas	Goodison and Wilson	2017	☐☐☐☐☐	⊘	◇◇◇
Los Angeles PD	California	McCluskey et al.	2019	☐☐☐	▲	◇◇◇◇◇◇
National survey	USA	Hamm et al.	2019	☐☐☐☐☐	▲	◇◇◇◇◇
Spokane PD	Washington	White et al.	2017	☐☐☐☐☐	▲	◇◇◇◇

☐ Level 1	▲ significant increase	◇ < 25 per group
☐☐ Level 2	△ increase	◇◇ 25–49 per group
☐☐☐ Level 3	▼ significant decrease	◇◇◇ 50–74 per group
☐☐☐☐ Level 4	▽ decrease	◇◇◇◇ 75–99 per group
☐☐☐☐☐ Level 5	⊘ null	◇◇◇◇◇ 100–499 per group
		◇◇◇◇◇◇ > 500 per group

the strongest. Level 5 studies are randomized controlled trials (RCTs), widely considered the gold standard in research. The next column provides a visual indicator of the study's summary findings: a down arrow for a decline in procedural justice, an up arrow for an increase in procedural justice, and a null sign for no statistical or substantive change. A solid arrow indicates that the change is statistically significant ($p < .05$). The final column illustrates the sample size per group.

Does the research show that BWCs improve police legitimacy through increased procedural justice? For the most part, yes. But the story is not clear-cut. Hamm and colleagues conducted a national survey in the United States.[27] Respondents who were randomly assigned to see an officer with a recording camera were significantly more likely to rate the officer's behavior as fair and procedurally just. Researchers in Anaheim (California), Arlington (Texas), and Spokane (Washington) conducted telephone surveys with citizens who had face-to-face encounters with police. They asked questions about the four elements of procedural justice and then analyzed the difference between officers with and without BWCs. Spokane was the only site where citizens were significantly more likely to report higher levels of procedurally just policing with BWCs.

The team in Los Angeles took a different approach and used systematic social observations (SSOs) to assess procedural justice. Researchers rode along with officers both before and one year after BWC deployment. Even with this different methodological approach, they found significantly higher levels of procedurally just policing once officers wore cameras.

Why did Anaheim and Arlington not experience the same benefit of BWCs? It is hard to say, but there could be a number of reasons. The Arlington researchers did not ask if the citizen was aware of the BWC and just reported whether the officer had a camera, whereas Anaheim and Spokane *only* counted an officer as a BWC officer if the member of the public was aware of the device. Findings from a London Metropolitan Police Service (MPS) study, however, cast doubt that these different methodologies actually influenced results.[28] Researchers with the MPS collected data on public attitudes toward BWC through a routine Public Attitude Survey (PAS). During the trial BWC implementation, over half (51 percent) of PAS respondents were not aware that MPS officers were wearing BWCs. There was no difference in levels of confidence toward police (one measure of legitimacy) among those who were aware and those who were not aware of the BWC. A study in Tempe (Arizona) reported the same finding.[29]

The Anaheim study is a bit more perplexing. Researchers failed to find significant differences despite accounting for citizen awareness of BWCs. This could be due to smaller group sizes ($N = 59$), or it could simply be that the cameras did not change procedurally just policing in this site. In Box 2.3, the captain in charge of BWC rollout in Anaheim reflects on the insignificant findings.

BOX 2.3

"Many departments believe that a body-worn camera program will increase the public's trust in their department and provide an increased sense of legitimacy and procedural justice during police contacts. We subscribe to the approach that the public's opinion of our department is primarily influenced by how our officers treat each person they contact. Trust, transparency, and mutual respect is earned by our officers' behavior, not by a recording device worn on their uniform."
—Captain Steve Marcin, Field Services Division Commander, Anaheim Police Department (authors' interview)

Summary

BWCs' ability to strengthen community trust in the police has been repeatedly identified by advocates of the technology. But this section reveals a muddy evidence base for this argument. Citizen and officer perception surveys, as well as a couple of systematic social observations,

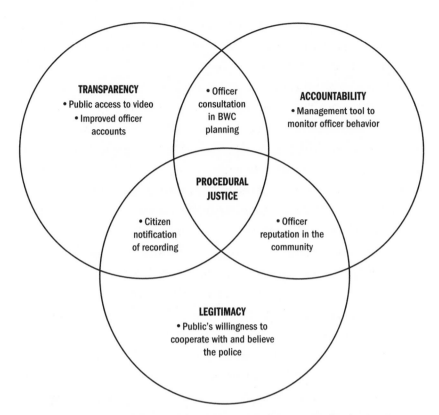

FIGURE 2.1. Conceptual frameworks and operational outcomes related to BWCs and trust

mostly tell the same story: BWCs increase police transparency, accountability, and legitimacy.

There are, however, several gaps in the research stemming from poor operationalization. Simply showing that citizens and officers support BWCs does not provide evidence that BWCs increase community trust. Also, asking citizens to define transparency, accountability, and legitimacy themselves is fraught with validity and reliability issues. To clarify what we mean, figure 2.1 illustrates the areas where more research is needed but also highlights the challenging overlaps and conceptual confusions surrounding transparency, accountability, and legitimacy.

The broad conceptual frameworks are highlighted in this idealized model in capital letters, while some of the potential operationalization issues are framed in lower case.

To better measure transparency, we need more research into *how* departments provide the public with access to video footage and how and if BWC footage improves officer incident accounts. A binary measure of whether a police department provides access is not sufficient, given the many hurdles that can influence access. Legitimacy research needs to focus on how BWCs affect the public's willingness to cooperate with and believe in the police. And research on how police management uses BWC footage to monitor officer behavior, most notably how BWCs affect the processes and outcomes of internal police investigations, would address a notable oversight in accountability research.

There are also research gaps that overlap more than one concept of trust. Further research is needed into whether notifying citizens that they are being recorded affects perceptions of transparency and legitimacy. Does citizen awareness of the BWC matter? Further research is also needed on how officer consultation into the BWC planning process affects officer buy-in. Finally, more research on how BWCs affect the reputation of officers in the community will help measure increased legitimacy and accountability. The next section reviews another purported strength of BWCs: the civilizing effect.

The "Civilizing Effect" of BWCs

Advocates argue BWCs have a civilizing effect on both citizens and officers, which leads to less use of force by police, fewer citizen complaints, less resistance by citizens, and as a consequence, fewer injuries and fatalities.[30] Notably, the majority of perception studies show that citizens believe BWCs will improve police officers' behavior.[31] For example, White and colleagues found that 76 percent of Spokane citizens they surveyed agreed that BWCs would cause officers to act more professionally; and 70 percent reported that BWCs would lead to more respectful behavior by citizens.[32] Perceptual studies show that officers are much more skeptical about the impact of BWCs on citizen behavior.[33] The "civilizing effect" claim is grounded in two theoretical frameworks, deterrence and self-awareness (see Box 2.4), which posit that people are more likely to behave in socially desirable ways if they know they are being observed.[34] This section begins by reviewing the rapidly growing body of research examining the impact of BWCs on use of force and then moves to research on BWCs and citizen complaints against officers.

BOX 2.4

"[Self-awareness theory] suggests that when human beings are under observation, they modify their behavior, exhibit more socially acceptable behavior, . . . and cooperate more fully with the rules. A well-developed line of research suggests that people do alter their behavior once they know that they are being observed."
—Anthony Braga et al., "Effects of Body-Worn Cameras" (2018)

The Impact of BWCs on Use of Force

Early research linked BWCs with dramatic reductions in use of force by police. As mentioned in chapter 1, the Rialto (California) Police Department study—the first-ever randomized controlled trial of BWCs—found a sharp drop in use of force associated with the rollout of BWCs. The Rialto study randomized shifts rather than officers, and Tony Farrar reported that "shifts without cameras experienced twice as many incidents of use of force as shifts with cameras."[35] Barak Ariel et al. provide a bit more detail on the use-of-force patterns in Rialto, noting that prior to BWCs, the department averaged approximately sixty-five use-of-force incidents per year. During the one-year BWC study, there were just twenty-five use-of-force incidents, seventeen during non-BWC shifts and eight during BWC shifts. Results from sophisticated regression modeling showed the reduction to be statistically significant.[36] Setting aside statistical significance, this year-to-year decline is quite remarkable, and not surprisingly, the Rialto study drew a significant amount of attention. Sutherland and colleagues recently tested whether the initial declines in Rialto have persisted, and they concluded, "This new evidence from Rialto tells us that the effects of cameras have been maintained long after the experiment concluded. Our interpretation of this is that the cameras and associated changes in police practice . . . once embedded as part of the experiment, simply became 'habit' for officers."[37]

From 2013 to 2018, a quickly growing body of research examined the impact of BWCs on officers' use of force. A handful of researchers have sought to summarize the findings from these BWC/use-of-force studies. Sander Flight conducted a metaevaluation of nine studies and reported, "Use of force by the police decreased in three of the nine evaluations, with an effect size ranging from a decrease of 28% up to a decrease of 75%. One study reported no change in use of force by the police. The other five evaluations did not contain information on use of force."[38] John Maskaly and colleagues conducted a review of twenty-one published BWC studies and concluded, "BWCs make officers less likely to use force."[39] Cynthia Lum and colleagues reviewed results from sixteen studies examining the impact of BWCs on use of force, and their conclusion was a bit more skeptical: "these study findings do not reveal a definitive conclusion that BWCs can reduce officers' use of force."[40] In May 2018, Michael White and colleagues released an "outcome directory" to concisely summarize the body of research in this area.[41]

We have summarized the use-of-force directory in table 2.2. Each published study is reflected in a row, and if an agency is the subject of multiple publications, each publication is listed separately (e.g., there are multiple Rialto entries). Importantly, each study's entry has been approved by the primary researcher or an independent expert to ensure accuracy. Similar to the table 2.1, each entry includes basic information

TABLE 2.2. Use-of-Force Research

Agency	Location	Authors	Year	Rigor	Finding	Sample size
Anonymous	USA	Koslicki et al.	2019	□□	▽	◇◇◇
Birmingham South PD	England	Henstock and Ariel	2017	□□□□□	◌	◇◇◇◇◇
Boston PD	Massachusetts	Braga et al.	2018	□□□□□	◌	◇◇◇◇◇
DC Metro PD	DC	Yokum et al.	2017	□□□□□	◌	◇◇◇◇◇◇
Denver PD	Colorado	Ariel	2016	□□□	◌	◇◇◇◇◇
Edmonton PS	Canada	Edmonton PS	2015	□□□	◌	◇◇◇
Hallandale Beach PD	Florida	Headley et al.	2017	□□□□	◌	◇◇
Las Vegas Metro PD	Nevada	Braga et al.	2017 2018	□□□□□	▼	◇◇◇◇◇
Miami PD	Florida	Chin-Quee	2018	□□	▼	◇◇◇◇
Miami-Dade PD	Florida	Stoltzenberg et al.	2019	□□	▼	◇◇◇◇◇◇
Milwaukee PD	Wisconsin	Peterson et al.	2018	□□□□□	◌	◇◇◇◇◇
Multisite	International	Ariel et al.	2016	□□□□□	◌	◇◇◇◇◇◇
Orlando PD	Florida	Jennings et al.	2015	□□□□□	▼	◇◇
Rialto PD	California	Sutherland et al.	2017	□□□□□	▽	◇◇◇◇◇
Rialto PD	California	Ariel et al.	2015	□□□□□	▼	◇◇◇◇◇
Rialto PD	California	Farrar	2013	□□□□□	▼	◇◇◇◇◇
Spokane PD	Washington	White et al.	2017	□□□□□	▽	◇◇◇◇
Tampa PD	Florida	Jennings et al.	2017	□□□	▼	◇◇◇
Toronto PS	Canada	Toronto PS	2016	□□□	▽	◇◇◇◇

□ Level 1	▲ significant increase	◇ < 25 per group
□□ Level 2	△ increase	◇◇ 25–49 per group
□□□ Level 3	▼ significant decrease	◇◇◇ 50–74 per group
□□□□ Level 4	▽ decrease	◇◇◇◇ 75–99 per group
□□□□□ Level 5	◌ null	◇◇◇◇◇ 100–499 per group
		◇◇◇◇◇◇ > 500 per group

about the study: the agency, the location, the researchers, the year of the publication, and the rigor of the study as determined by its rating on the SMS. The next column provides a visual indicator of the study's summary findings, using the same scale described in table 2.1: a down arrow for a decline in use of force, an up arrow for an increase in use of force, and null sign for no statistical or substantive change. A solid arrow indicates the change is statistically significant ($p < .05$), and a white arrow indicates the authors reported notable declines in use of force but the decline was not statistically significant. Given that use of force is a rare event in most agencies, reaching the level of statistical significance is often difficult even when there is a large decline. The online directory also indicates whether the documented change was measured through a between-group analysis (BWC group compared to non-BWC group) or a within-group analysis (one group over time, pre- and post-BWC deployment), as well as the percentage change for the between- and within-group comparisons.

An example will help demonstrate the use of table 2.2. The Orlando (Florida) Police Department participated in a research study with researchers Wesley Jennings and colleagues. The study was published in 2015 and is a level 5 on the SMS (RCT). The finding column indicates a statistically significant decline in use of force after implementing BWCs (black down arrow). If you follow up on this study in the online directory, you will find that the between-group analysis determined use of force was 26 percent lower among BWC officers, compared to non-BWC officers, though this difference does not reach statistical significance. According to the within-group analysis, both groups experienced statistically significant declines from pre- to post-BWC deployment: the frequency of force declined 53 percent for the BWC group and 38 percent for the non-BWC group (both of which reached statistical significance).

There are a few important takeaways from table 2.2. First, the majority of studies were conducted with departments in the United States (fifteen of nineteen). Second, eleven of the nineteen studies were randomized, controlled trials. The prevalence of RCTs is extraordinary, and it is unlikely that there is another area in policing research where a body of rigorous studies has accumulated so quickly. This is a testament to both the researchers and the agencies that participated in the studies. Third, eleven of the studies documented declines in use of force, and seven of the eleven reductions were statistically significant. Those declines occurred in studies with the Las Vegas Metropolitan Police Department, the Miami-Dade Police Department, the Orlando Police Department, the Rialto Police Department, the Spokane Police Department, the Tampa Police Department, and the Toronto Police Service. The declines in use of force have been documented through within-group analysis, between-group analysis, or both. Notably, just one of the non-US studies documented notable reductions in use of force. Last, none of the studies provide insights into why there were reductions in officer use of force. Did citizens improve their behavior, leading to less use of force by officers? Or perhaps citizen behavior remained the same and officer behavior changed. Or maybe even behavior change occurred among both citizens and officers. The current studies do not shed light on the underlying causes of reductions in use of force by police (when those reductions occur).

The Impact of BWCs on Citizen Complaints

Reductions in citizen complaints—and decreased time for investigating complaints—have been central to the purported benefits of BWCs. The Rialto study, for example, documented a nearly 90 percent reduction in citizen complaints following BWC deployment,[42] and those effects have persisted.[43] The meta-evaluations conducted by Flight and Maskaly et al. both concluded BWCs lead to reductions in complaints against officers.[44] Flight reported, "The number of complaints against the police decreased according to five of the nine studies. The effect size ranged from a 14% decrease to an 87% decrease."[45] Lum and colleagues concur, noting that "researchers have mostly found that officers wearing BWCs receive fewer reported complaints than do those that are not wearing the cameras."[46] (Table 2.3 summarizes the research for citizen complaints.)[47]

Table 2.3 and the online citizen complaint directory can be interpreted in the same way as the use-of-force directory, and the Orlando entry can again be used to illustrate. The Orlando Police Department participated in a research study with Jennings and his research colleagues. The

TABLE 2.3. Complaint Research

Agency	Location	Authors	Year	Rigor	Finding	Sample size
Anonymous	USA	Koen et al.	2018	□□	▽	◇◇◇
Arlington PD	Texas	Goodison and Wilson	2017	□□□□□	▽	◇◇◇◇
Boston PD	Massachusetts	Braga et al.	2018	□□□□□	⊘	◇◇◇◇◇
DC Metro PD	DC	Yokum et al.	2017	□□□□□	⊘	◇◇◇◇◇◇
Denver PD	Colorado	Ariel	2016	□□□	▼	◇◇◇◇◇
Edmonton PS	Canada	Edmonton PS	2015	□□□	⊘	◇◇◇
Hallandale Beach PD	Florida	Headley et al.	2017	□□□□	⊘	◇◇
Isle of Wight Constabulary	England and Wales	Ellis et al.	2015	□□□	▽	◇◇◇◇◇
Las Vegas Metro PD	Nevada	Braga, Coldren, et al.	2017 2018	□□□□□	▼	◇◇◇◇
London Metro PD	England	Grossmith et al.	2015	□□□□□	▼	◇◇◇◇◇◇
Mesa PD	Arizona	Mesa PD	2013	□□□□	▽	◇◇◇
Milwaukee PD	Wisconsin	Peterson et al.	2018	□□□□□	▽	◇◇◇◇◇
Multisite	International	Ariel et al.	2017	□□□□□	▽	◇◇◇◇◇◇
Miami PD	Florida	Chin-Quee	2018	□□	▼	◇◇◇◇
Miami-Dade PD	Florida	Stoltzenberg et al.	2019	□□	▼	◇◇◇◇◇◇
Orlando PD	Florida	Jennings et al.	2015	□□□□□	▼	◇◇
Phoenix PD	Arizona	Hedberg et al.	2017	□□□□	▼	◇◇◇
Phoenix PD	Arizona	Katz et al.	2014	□□□□	▼	◇◇◇
Plymouth Constabulary	England	Goodall	2007	□□	▽	◇◇◇◇◇
Rialto PD	California	Sutherland et al.	2017	□□□□□	▽	◇◇◇◇
Rialto PD	California	Ariel et al.	2015	□□□□□	▽	◇◇◇◇◇
Rialto PD	California	Farrar	2013	□□□□□	▽	◇◇◇◇◇
Republic of Uruguay	Uruguay	Mitchell et al.	2018	□□□□	▼	◇◇◇◇◇
Spokane PD	Washington	White et al.	2017	□□□□□	▽	◇◇◇◇
Toronto PS	Canada	Toronto PS	2016	□□□	▲	◇◇◇◇

□ Level 1	▲ significant increase	◇ < 25 per group
□□ Level 2	△ increase	◇◇ 25–49 per group
□□□ Level 3	▼ significant decrease	◇◇◇ 50–74 per group
□□□□ Level 4	▽ decrease	◇◇◇◇ 75–99 per group
□□□□□ Level 5	⊘ null	◇◇◇◇◇ 100–499 per group
		◇◇◇◇◇◇ > 500 per group

study was published in 2015 and again is an RCT (level 5 on the SMS). The finding column indicates a statistically significant decline in citizen complaints after BWC deployment, and the decline was documented in both the between-group and within-group analysis. More specifically, the between-group column in the online directory shows that the frequency of complaints is 53 percent lower among BWC officers, compared to non-BWC officers, and this decline reached statistical significance. The within-group column shows declines in complaints for both groups: a statistically significant 65 percent reduction in complaints for BWC officers and a 37 percent reduction for non-BWC officers (not statistically significant).

There are again a few important takeaways from table 2.3. Much like with the use-of-force directory, the majority of studies were conducted with departments in the United States (eighteen of twenty-five), and almost half were carried out as randomized, controlled trials (twelve of twenty-five). With regard to impact on complaints, twenty of the twenty-five studies have documented notable declines in complaints following the deployment of BWCs (nine documented statistically significant declines). Those declines have occurred in studies of departments in both the United States (anonymous, Arlington, Denver, Las Vegas, Mesa, Miami, Milwaukee, Orlando, Phoenix, Rialto, and Spokane) and the United Kingdom (Isle of Wight, London, multisite, and Plymouth). The declines in complaints have been documented through within-group analysis, between-group analysis, or both. In plain terms, the findings reported in table 2.3 are powerful. The current body of research strongly demonstrates that police BWCs lead to reductions in citizen complaints against police. Much like the use-of-force studies, the research on citizen complaints does not shed light on the causes of reductions in complaints. Do BWCs produce better behavior among officers, which leads to fewer complaints? Or perhaps the improved behavior of citizens is the underlying cause. Certainly, some portion of the reduction in complaints is explained by changes in citizen reporting patterns, specifically with regard to frivolous complaints. That is, citizens are less likely to file a false

complaint when they realize there is audio and video footage of the encounter that would directly refute their untruthful claim.[48]

Factors That Can Explain the Mixed Findings

The body of research examining the impact of BWCs on use of force and
complaints against officers is persuasive, especially for complaints, but
the findings are by no means unanimous. Not every study documented a
drop in those outcomes. Some studies showed a decline in one outcome
but not the other. The size of declines, when they occurred, also varied, with some reaching statistical significance but others not. The mixed
results on use of force and complaints have been troubling to some people
(see the media headlines in Box 1.3), and researchers have not sufficiently
explained the variation. We believe the mixed evidence base on the effect
of BWCs is explained, at least in part, by three factors: the agency starting
point, planning and implementation, and research-related issues.

THE STATE OF THE AGENCY PRE-BWC DEPLOYMENT

One key factor involves a given department's starting point. We raised
this issue in chapter 1. What was the state of the department prior to
BWC deployment? Has the department recently experienced a scandal or controversial event? Is the department under federal oversight
through a consent decree? Does the department have the necessary
accountability mechanisms in place to ensure professionalism among
officers? This starting point varies substantially among departments and
is likely to be critically important for interpreting the impact of BWCs.
For example, the Rialto Police Department had experienced a significant
misconduct scandal prior to hiring a new "reform chief," who, among
other efforts to improve the department, implemented a body-worn
camera program.[49] In effect, the Rialto Police Department was at a low
point when the BWC program started.

The Las Vegas Metropolitan and Spokane Police Departments implemented BWC programs following their involvement in Collaborative

Reform. Collaborative Reform is a US Department of Justice technical assistance mechanism available to law enforcement agencies that "offers recommendations based on a comprehensive agency assessment for how to resolve . . . issues and enhance the relationship between the police and the community."[50] In effect, the Las Vegas Metropolitan and Spokane Police Departments had proactively sought out federal assistance to identify problems and had implemented reforms to address those problems prior to deploying BWCs. The Washington, DC, Metropolitan Police Department, on the other hand, had been under a federal consent decree for nearly a decade during the early 2000s. The Washington, DC, BWC evaluators point to this experience under federal oversight as a potential explanation for the lack of an impact on use of force and complaints: "These reforms were implemented under DOJ oversight, which was terminated in 2008 at the recommendation of the Independent Monitor based on 'MPD's having achieved substantial compliance with the vast majority of the MOA's [memorandum of agreement's] 126 substantial provisions and requirements.' A subsequent audit of MPD's performance was conducted in 2015 at the request of the Office of the District of Columbia Auditor (ODCA), and found that the department has maintained its compliance with the 2001 MOA, with the reforms still in place."[51]

Given the variation in local context, is it a surprise that, post-BWC deployment, the Rialto Police Department experienced immediate, large declines in use of force and citizen complaints, while the Washington, DC, Metropolitan Police Department did not? Scandal-ridden agencies often are characterized by organizational deficiencies that lead to excessive and unnecessary force, high levels of citizen complaints, and low reserves of police legitimacy. Perhaps the large reductions in use of force and citizen complaints experienced by the Rialto Police Department were a reflection of the poor state of the agency prior to Chief Farrar's arrival and decision to deploy BWCs. Alternatively, professional organizations with restrictively high selection standards, robust training, effective supervision, and proper accountability systems do not experience those same negative outcomes because they were never in a bad place from which to recover. Perhaps the decade of federal oversight addressed the organizational deficiencies in the Washington, DC, Metro Police Department, prior to BWC deployment. There were no large reductions in use of force and citizen complaints because there did not need to be—officers were using appropriate levels of force already. In simple terms, troubled agencies that adopt BWCs may see the Rialto-like declines in use of force and citizen complaints because there is much room for improvement. Academic researchers would call this an endogeneity issue, where there is an important unmeasured variable, that of the agency starting point. To put it more bluntly, we may need to measure the starting point of a department because professional agencies have much less room for improvement. Such agencies are already functioning at a high level.

PLANNING AND IMPLEMENTATION

The mixed force and complaints findings may also be explained by the difficulties associated with BWC program implementation, which are considerable. BWCs require a tremendous investment of internal resources. BWCs affect every aspect of police operations and have implications for numerous stakeholders outside the police department. BWCs touch on a number of sensitive issues such as citizen privacy, public records laws, and recording of vulnerable populations.[52] Additionally, in many jurisdictions BWCs have been adopted in a contentious political environment following a controversial incident, which produces pressure to deploy the technology quickly. Recall that the Ferguson Police Department deployed cameras less than a month after Michael Brown's death.[53] These difficulties are compounded by the consequences of poor BWC program implementation, from resistance among line officers and unions and low BWC activation rates to problems with technology integration, data storage, and unintended costs (financial and otherwise).[54]

Consider officer BWC activation rates as a metric of implementation success. There have been a few studies examining activation rates, and the results indicate that activation compliance is quite challenging. Dave McClure et al. reported substantial variation in officer activation rates, from under 2 percent to more than 65 percent.[55] In Phoenix, Charles Katz et al. reported officer activation over time and by charge type.[56] Overall, activation compliance was approximately 30 percent, though it declined substantially over time. Low activation compliance is a form of implementation failure. In fact, Eric Hedberg and colleagues used sophisticated analysis to project the impact of BWCs on citizen complaints, had activation compliance been higher: "if BWCs are employed as prescribed [i.e., 100 percent activation compliance], a majority of complaints against officers would be eliminated."[57] In short, BWC implementation comes with both a high degree of difficulty and significant risks if implemented poorly. Poor implementation will short-circuit the potential for positive outcomes related to use of force and citizen complaints. We address BWC implementation in greater detail in chapter 5.

RESEARCH-RELATED ISSUES

A handful of decisions made by researchers can also affect the likelihood of documenting positive effects. First, how rigorous is the study? Where does it rank on the Maryland Scale of Scientific Methods (SMS)? Does the study have a non-BWC comparison group? Are the outcomes measured before and after BWC deployment or just after? Little confidence can be placed in results from studies that score less than level 3 on the SMS. Second, how do the researchers measure their outcomes? Do citizen complaints and use of force come from official department data, officer self-report, or some other source? Also, how long is the study period? Is there a meaningful period of time under observation both before and after the BWC deployment? The bottom line is that not all research studies are created equal. The degree of confidence placed in a study's findings should be directly proportional to its methodological rigor.

Even the most rigorous studies, randomized controlled trials (level 5), may have issues. In an RCT, there are treatment (BWC) and control (non-BWC) conditions, and the traditional approach is to randomize officers to those conditions. The randomization process allows one to assume that the two groups are similar in all respects except that one group received

BWCs (treatment group) and the other group did not (control group). As a result, any difference in outcomes can be attributed to the intervention, in this case, the BWC. The same principles apply to pharmaceutical trials that test new medications. You have an intervention (medication) and patients randomly assigned to two groups—one receives the medication and the other does not. Any change in the health of patients can then be attributed to the medication. Medical trials are conducted in controlled or even laboratory settings to eliminate the potential for a patient in the control group to receive the intervention or medication.

BWC studies are not conducted in a controlled setting, however, and officers in the treatment (BWC) and control (non-BWC) groups may interact regularly. They may see each other in the locker room, at roll calls, and on meal breaks. And BWC and non-BWC officers may respond to the same call. When that occurs, the non-BWC officer is "exposed" to the intervention (the BWC). This exposure, called "contamination" or "treatment spillover" in research terms, represents a violation of the integrity of the RCT design. More specifically, each control group exposure to a BWC reduces the potential to document a treatment effect because the control officer's behavior may now be changed by that exposure (just like a control group patient taking the experimental drug rather than the placebo).

Several researchers have documented a degree of contamination in their study. In the DC Metro study, 70 percent of the calls were contaminated.[58] In other words, a treatment effect could reasonably be expected in only 30 percent of the calls during the study period. The null findings in the DC Metro study may be explained, at least in part, by the large percentage of control officers who were exposed to BWCs. This mainly happened when non-BWC officers in the control group attended calls and crime scenes that were also attended by officers who were wearing cameras. How can we expect BWCs to affect the behavior of one group of officers (treatment) and not the other (control) when both groups are exposed to the technology? Contamination rates can vary considerably. For example, in the Las Vegas study, the researchers documented a contamination rate of approximately 20 percent.[59] Danielle Wallace and colleagues documented a 49 percent contamination rate in Spokane.[60]

Some researchers have sought to avoid the contamination problem by randomizing shifts rather than officers (e.g., Ariel's studies in Rialto and elsewhere). As a result, all officers working a given shift are in the same group: they either have BWCs, or they do not. This approach on its face seems to remove the potential contamination. However, one could argue that the contamination in this kind of design is actually 100 percent, as every officer in the study bounces back and forth between the treatment and control conditions. One week an officer has a BWC; the next week the same officer does not. In effect, each officer is exposed to the intervention. This would be like each patient in a pharmaceutical trial intermittently taking both a placebo and the experimental drug. It becomes nearly impossible to isolate the effect of the drug on patient health.

Ariel and colleagues refer to the issue in terms of a violation of the Stable Unit Treatment Value Assumption (SUTVA), and they make a compelling case for the problems with treatment spillover in an officer-based randomization, using the DC Metro study as a case study.[61] Ariel and colleagues acknowledge the problems with a shift-based randomization, but they advocate for the approach as a "least worst option" because it allows researchers to increase sample sizes and better understand SUTVA violations.[62] We believe there is no simple answer to the question of the proper unit of analysis in BWC RCTs. In some cases, a shift-based randomization is the optimal approach. However, some police departments may push back against such an approach because the leadership prefers the certainties associated with a more traditional officer-based randomization (e.g., at any given time, the chief knows who has a BWC and who does not). Department size and the number of BWCs deployed can also play a role in the potential contamination problem. If a department has 500 officers, the deployment of 250 BWCs presents a larger contamination problem than does the deployment of 100 BWCs in the same department.[63] In very large departments, the contamination problem can be minimized by a cluster-RCT, where BWCs are randomized to some precincts but not to others. If BWC and non-BWC precincts are not adjacent, there will be very little opportunity for contamination. Of course, very few police departments are large enough to accommodate such a randomization approach (e.g., the New York City Police Department).

Interestingly, the potential for contamination is a research problem but not necessarily a police problem. If the goal of the BWC program is to reduce citizen complaints, and all officers (BWC and non-BWC) experience a reduction because they were all exposed to BWCs, then all the better for the police department. The department achieved its objective regardless of the concerns over research design integrity. Ariel et al. describe this phenomenon as a natural process: "We argue that that BWCs affect entire police departments through a process we label *contagious accountability*. Whatever the precise mechanism of the deterrence effect of being watched and, by implication, accountability, all officers in the departments were acutely aware of being observed more closely, with an enhanced transparency apparatus that has never been seen before in day-to-day policing operations. Everyone was affected by it, even when the cameras were not in use, and collectively everyone in the department(s) attracted fewer complaints."[64]

Summary

The mixed findings regarding the impact of BWCs on use of force and citizen complaints may result from a number of issues. The state of an agency pre-BWC deployment matters. Planning and implementation matter. Research design matters. Efforts by researchers to summarize the body of knowledge in this area are important, but researchers also must begin to dig deeper to explain variation in findings across studies.

Evidentiary Value: BWC Use in Investigations

Another benefit of BWCs is their ability to improve evidence collected in police investigations. In fact, this is reported as one of the main reasons departments choose to buy cameras and can help sell a BWC program to reluctant officers and unions (see Box 2.5).[65] We elaborate more on the challenge of police union buy-in in chapter 3. BWCs provide a much more accurate account of incidents than does traditional written reporting, limited only by the video and audio range of the cameras. These benefits are supported anecdotally by officers, prosecutors, and judges (see Box 2.6), but more rigorous evidence supporting these claims is scant.

BOX 2.5

"Our Department viewed body-worn cameras (BWC) as a tremendous evidence-collection tool, and we saw our BWC program as a way to increase efficiency and effectiveness. With body-worn cameras, behavior descriptions such as intoxicated, irrational, aggressive, or distraught would be memorialized for juries to see for themselves. Environmental conditions, distances, fields of view, interviews, and police actions could all be viewed instead of relying on written descriptions and after-incident photographs. These capabilities would dramatically increase our officers' ability to present a more comprehensive investigation, justify their actions, and substantiate their perspectives. This was how we presented body-worn cameras as we initiated our implementation. The value of BWCs to collect evidence became so apparent so quickly, we had units begin using their cameras ahead of our implementation schedule."
—Captain Steve Marcin, Field Services Division Commander, Anaheim Police Department (authors' interview)

BOX 2.6

"We had a rape case where the police report stated the victim was upset. When we played the tape in getting ready for trial, 'upset' was an understatement—she was crying uncontrollably as the responding officers were trying to get information about the violent stranger

> rape that had just occurred. As you would expect, when she took the stand at trial, she was composed and reluctant to show emotion. The judge and jury then got to see her on the videos, and some cried too as the tape was being played. Preserving that raw impact a crime has on a victim is very powerful and is useful evidence to accurately portray to the jury what happened those many months ago. Victims and witnesses will downplay or wall off the raw emotion of an event when months or years pass before they testify, but having on-scene video of their reactions the day of the crime is extremely useful for prosecutors."
> —Damon Mosler, Deputy District Attorney, San Diego County District Attorney's Office (authors' interview)

Citizen Complaints

Not only do BWCs minimize doubts about citizen behavior, but they can also be used in the investigation of complaints against officers (see Box 2.7). Only a few studies have examined how the investigative value of BWCs affects the processing of citizen complaints. Katz and colleagues reported that officers with BWCs were more likely to be exonerated from citizen complaints, compared to their colleagues without BWCs.[66] Braga and colleagues completed a cost-benefit analysis of the Las Vegas Metropolitan Police Department, and they reported cost savings of nearly $4 million per year.[67] The vast majority of that cost savings came as a result of reduced investigative time and resources devoted to citizen complaints.

BOX 2.7

"We had a motorcycle traffic officer stop a mom with her eight-year-old daughter in an affluent part of the county. The officer fortunately was equipped with a camera. The driver became argumentative and

refused to sign the ticket. She berated the officer and started to make false accusations when her first approach did not work. She called 911 and proceeded to allege all kinds of misconduct by the officer. He tells her that he has a camera and is taping. She keeps on the call with 911 alleging he has touched her and is physical with her—all false. She gets arrested for refusing to sign the citation. When she goes to court, her attorney has the 911 call and claims to the court that the officer engaged in misconduct. The officer lets the prosecutor know there is BWC evidence. The case is continued, and when the video is retrieved, the entire case turns around: she pleads guilty and has to apologize to the officer and his command. Without that tape the outcome might have been quite different, and the officer could have been disciplined, if not fired."
—Damon Mosler, Deputy District Attorney, San Diego County District Attorney's Office (authors' interview)

Criminal Investigations

In a national survey of prosecutors about BWCs, Linda Merola and colleagues found that 80 percent support BWC use and 63 percent feel the footage will assist prosecutions more than defense.[68] A majority of lead prosecutors (66 percent) agreed that BWCs would improve their overall ability to prosecute cases. Also of note, only 8 percent of prosecutors who had video footage available used it in cases against officers. Therefore, it makes sense that all of the evidence in this area pertains to citizen criminal investigations and not in cases of officer misconduct. But for all this, research in this area is still pretty thin, with only eight published studies (see table 2.4).

The eight studies focus on a couple of different evidentiary benefits: the effect on detection of crime and arrests and whether BWCs affect case outcomes. Four of the studies are from the United Kingdom and have limited methodological rigor, with three of them falling at level 3 or below in the SMS.[69] These studies show that BWCs increase detection of crime, arrests, and guilty pleas. Other research suggests that camera

TABLE 2.4. Criminal Investigation Research

Agency	Location	Authors	Year	Rigor	Finding	Sample size
Aberdeen and Renfrewshire	Scotland	ODS Consulting	2011	□□	△	◊◊◊
DC Metro PD	DC	Yokum et al.	2017	□□□□□	⊘	◊◊◊◊◊◊
Essex Constabulary	England	Owens et al.	2014	□□□□□	▲	◊◊◊◊◊
Isle of Wight Constabulary	England and Wales	Ellis et al.	2015	□□□	△	◊◊◊◊◊
Phoenix PD	Arizona	Morrow et al. Katz et al.	2016 2014	□□□□	△	◊◊◊
Plymouth Constabulary	England	Goodall	2007	□□	△	◊◊◊◊◊
Tempe PD	Arizona	White et al.	2019	□□□□□	⊘	◊◊◊◊◊

□ Level 1	▲ significant increase	◊ < 25 per group
□□ Level 2	△ increase	◊◊ 25–49 per group
□□□ Level 3	▼ significant decrease	◊◊◊ 50–74 per group
□□□□ Level 4	▽ decrease	◊◊◊◊ 75–99 per group
□□□□□ Level 5	⊘ null	◊◊◊◊◊ 100–499 per group
		◊◊◊◊◊◊ > 500 per group

footage is particularly beneficial for incidents with less cooperative victims, such as domestic violence.[70] Researchers implementing an RCT in Essex (United Kingdom) found that domestic violence investigations with BWC footage were significantly more likely to result in a criminal charge.[71] Officers from the study report that this could be due to BWCs' ability capture the emotions and injuries present at the scene, whether or not victims recant their statement. Researchers working with the Phoenix Police Department found that domestic violence cases with BWC footage are more likely to result in a guilty plea or verdict.[72]

However, as we have seen before, not all research tells the same story. In the DC Metro RCT, Yokum et al. found no difference in either the rate of prosecution or possible dispositions.[73] The difference between the DC study and the larger body of research is probably due to the same reasons discussed in the use of force and citizen complaints section: contextual differences between DC and other sites and the high level of contamination. Michael White and colleagues found no difference in guilty dispositions, but did find a significant reduction in time to adjudication when BWC evidence was available.[74] Overall, though, the limited evidence suggests that BWCs do improve criminal investigations. Lum and colleagues concur with our assessment, as they conclude, "the findings from stronger studies also reveal that BWCs have investigative benefits."[75]

Training Value and Sentinel Events Review

If BWCs are to positively change police behavior and performance, this is most likely to come through training and sentinel events review.[76] BWC footage captures information that is usually not in police reports. Reports document results, while video footage documents how events transpired; in effect, traditional police reporting prioritizes the ends over the means. By reviewing video, departments can identify both tactical errors and exemplary practice. They can then use the footage to isolate gaps in training (see Box 2.8). The Linden, New Jersey, Police Department tried to do just that. They reviewed reports and civil lawsuits and identified the top-five incident types that were causing the agency "the most trouble."[77] BWC footage in each of these incident types was reviewed, and training was designed to reform the department. But like most department-initiated reforms, no rigorous evaluation exists to empirically assess whether the Linden Police Department's efforts actually improved police behavior and performance. Unfortunately, the use of video footage in training and sentinel events review is one of the most understudied areas of BWC research.

BOX 2.8

"In addition to the standard training benefits once BWCs have been implemented, there are ways to utilize them beyond the understood or perceived. Imagination and thinking creatively allow you to use BWCs for virtually any training. Use of actual incidents for the good,

the bad, the ugly, or to demonstrate a 'best practice' can be one of your most valuable tools. Utilizing BWC's for defensive tactics, use of force, active shooter, deescalation, and beyond can be limitless. Summed up in two words, think creatively."
—Geoffrey D. Smith, Director of Public Safety, City of Sturgis (Michigan) (authors' interview)

Only three studies have examined how BWCs impact police training. Joshua Phelps et al. conducted a quasi-experimental study with the Norwegian Police University College to examine how BWCs were used in decision reflection.[78] The researchers used BWCs attached to the subjects' protective glasses and recorded their activity during training simulations. The video was replayed for the subjects to analyze and reflect on their performance in the areas of communication, decision-making, coping with stress, and police tactics. The researchers found that officers trained on BWCs were more likely than those without the training to identify mistakes and reflect on learning experiences. Marthinus Koen et al. conducted a retrospective interview study with twenty-three officers in a small US police department and asked how BWCs influenced decision-making, performance evaluations, and training.[79] The officers were also each observed for approximately two hours to learn about the cameras in their natural setting. The officers reported that videos could be useful for training, but in practice BWC footage was not central to how trainers instructed and evaluated recruits. The Toronto Police Service conducted a quasi-experimental study incorporating BWC scenario-based training.[80] They found BWCs to be useful in an initial training capacity, but the authors gave no indication as to whether ongoing training incorporating BWC footage exists.

It is obvious from this review that the potential for BWCs in police training is tremendous, but much more research is needed. Future research should focus on whether BWC footage can help officers learn and retain concepts and skills better and, perhaps even more importantly, whether this education has a measurable effect on officer behavior.

Conclusion

This chapter has reviewed the evidence on the many claims made about the benefits of BWCs. The research base on BWCs has grown rapidly in the past five years, and a significant number of the available studies are methodologically rigorous. As a result, we can have some confidence in drawing conclusions about the impact of BWCs. Clearly, a significant number of police departments have experienced positive results after deploying BWCs, from reductions in use of force and citizen complaints to improvements in citizen perceptions of procedural justice and enhanced evidentiary value. At the same time, other studies show none of those benefits, and we have offered some initial thoughts on potential explanations for that variation. These include the state of an agency predeployment, aspects of planning and implementation, and research-related issues. The claims explored in this chapter, however, represent only half the story. In chapter 3, we review the challenges and limitations associated with BWCs.

3

The Challenges and Limitations of Body-Worn Cameras

While BWCs have gained strong support over the past five years, they also have their share of skeptics. Critics argue that a host of BWC costs outweigh the benefits, costs such as loss of privacy, excessive financial burden, tension between officers and management, and reduced police activity. The challenges do not stop there. Agencies implementing the technology have to develop detailed policies that further complicate police work. And departments need to work with external stakeholders to ensure the footage generated by BWCs is utilized throughout the criminal justice system. Therefore, even though chapter 2 revealed important benefits of BWCs, they are not a panacea. BWCs will not remedy years of antagonism between police and the community. BWCs will not necessarily lessen tension between the department leadership and the rank and file. And BWCs will not automatically increase the likelihood of successful prosecution. As we have stated throughout the book, BWCs come with a very high degree of difficulty, and if implemented poorly, a BWC program can actually make matters worse.

In this chapter, we provide an overview of evidence on the challenges and limitations of BWCs. Just like chapter 2, we use graphical tables to illustrate research findings where possible and integrate officer vignettes to bring a combination of evidence-based and practitioner-led insights. We start by discussing citizen and officer privacy issues. We then explore the very limited research examining cost and resource issues. No discussion of BWC challenges would be complete without examining the internal challenges of BWC programs, especially designing an effective BWC policy. Another issue that has made headlines is the possibility of BWCs creating a depolicing effect, in which police reduce their proactivity. We review research in the area of police activity to assess this claim.

Finally, we review one of the most overlooked areas in BWC research: the importance of external stakeholder commitment and coordination. Overall, our intent with chapters 2 and 3 is to present a balanced review of the issues and the evidence. This balanced review sets the stage for the final two chapters, which begin to look forward (rather than back) with this technology.

Citizen and Officer Privacy Issues

Every benefit can have a cost; and in the case of BWCs, the cost of increased transparency is decreased privacy. The question of how to balance transparency and confidentiality has elicited several different opinions. Some citizen groups call for BWC policies that mandate officers never turn off their cameras while on duty.[1] Privacy rights groups, such as the American Civil Liberties Union (ACLU), believe the majority of BWC video should not be available to the public. They note that exceptions should exist where "there is a strong public interest in that video that outweighs privacy concerns: where there is a use of force, or a complaint against an officer."[2] Police departments try to thread a needle by constructing policies that somehow accommodate these two opposing views, while abiding by state privacy legislation. It is not an easy task. In this section, we describe both citizen and officer privacy concerns and review the limited research investigating this highly contentious issue.

Citizen Privacy

BWCs infringe on citizen privacy in a multitude of ways. They record sensitive information, at a time when citizens—offenders, victims, or even bystanders—are usually at their worst. The public release of this information could be emotionally damaging or even dangerous to the citizens recorded. Fear concerning officers recording and releasing the actions and communications of members of the public might also reduce the willingness of the public to report crime or give witness statements.

For all of these reasons, departments need to develop policies that not only protect citizens' right to privacy and limit who can view the recording but also promote transparency (see Box 3.1).

BOX 3.1

"If BWC video is under consideration of being released to the public, the needs of the legal system, the desires of the family, and the demands of the community must somehow be balanced in the decision of how and when to release video."
—Carolyn Naoroz, Body-Worn Camera Administrative Project Analyst, Richmond, Virginia, Police Department (authors' interview)

There are a host of surveys asking citizens about BWCs and privacy concerns. And just like the research presented in chapter 2, the findings are not clear. Matthew Crow and colleagues surveyed residents of two Florida counties and found that respondents were not overly concerned about privacy, with only 11 percent agreeing or strongly agreeing that BWCs are an invasion of citizen privacy.[3] Lynne Grossmith and colleagues surveyed both officers and citizens in London, United Kingdom, and found a similar disregard for citizen privacy issues.[4] However, the Toronto Police Service found that citizens reported a lower likelihood of speaking informally to officers wearing BWCs.[5] In another Canadian study, the Edmonton Police Service reported a contradiction between two different citizen survey populations.[6] It found the general population to have greater privacy concerns than citizens who had face-to-face contact with BWC officers. In Australia, Emmeline Taylor and colleagues interviewed citizens held in custody and asked why BWCs were *not* a good idea; the most common response was privacy issues (21 percent).[7] These mixed results reflect the challenges in this area and mirror research that dives further into the effect of privacy concerns on citizen behavior.

Crime detection and clearance rates have been declining for some years. The last thing departments probably want to introduce is technology that further reduces one of their key performance metrics, citizen cooperation. For this reason alone, it is useful to study if BWCs will affect victim, witness, and even offender cooperation with police. However, only a handful of studies examine how BWCs influence citizen attitudes about privacy and willingness to engage with police. The Edmonton Police Service's public survey found that people were still willing to provide information to police, despite BWCs.[8] The Toronto Police Service interviewed citizens encountering the police and found that BWCs made individuals less likely to talk to officers, though this only held true for suspects or witnesses, not victims of crime.[9] Only one study directly explored the effect of BWCs on citizen cooperation, rather than the self-reported perception of cooperation: Grossmith and colleagues found that the presence of a BWC had no impact on two measures of cooperation—victims who were unwilling to prosecute and insufficient evidence to proceed.[10]

Officer Privacy

Citizens are not the only population to experience privacy issues with the spread of BWCs; officers also have concerns. For the most part, officers have come to appreciate the benefits of BWCs; however, it is worth remembering that we are asking officers to record their daily activities on the job. And while this is not completely new territory for the police (consider in-car video and voice recorders), it is unreasonable to assume this invasion of privacy would come without at least mild apprehension. At present, however, this appears to be of relatively little concern to the community. Crow and colleagues reported that less than 10 percent of the general population agreed or strongly agreed that the cameras are an invasion of officer privacy.[11] Officers however, do worry about supervisors going on "fishing expeditions" and reviewing footage just to catch an officer violating policy.[12] They are also uneasy about the possibility of BWCs capturing personal conversations and activities. The Toronto Police Service reported that almost half of its officers were not certain the department's BWC policy protected their privacy.[13]

What can departments do to address these concerns? Moreover, does the inevitable impact on officer privacy affect police activities? Unfortunately, research addressing both questions is almost nonexistent. There have been a couple of studies that have reviewed officer privacy policies and made suggestions for best practices. The Police Executive Research Forum (PERF) released a report on BWC model policies and recommended that agencies should "prohibit recording other agency personnel during routine, non-enforcement-related activities unless recording is required by a court order or is authorized as part of an administrative or criminal investigation."[14] Most departments have taken this advice and produced policies specifying where BWCs should not be activated.[15] Michael White and colleagues found that nearly all BWC policies they reviewed from 2015 to 2017 identified recording privacy restrictions.[16] These policies prohibited recording privileged conversations (e.g., attorney, spouse, and confidential sources) and in locations with an expectation of privacy (such as locker rooms and restrooms). In the United States at least, it is important to mention that BWC footage is considered a public record and can normally be obtained through public records requests.[17] States have dramatically different public records legislation, so each department must educate itself on these laws and then attempt to protect officer privacy while still abiding by the relevant statutes.

In addition to policy formation, White suggests that police leadership should explain the goals and objectives of a department's BWC program at implementation and then respond to officer concerns.[18] For instance, in Anaheim (California), the leadership team worked with the union to identify officer privacy concerns. Representatives from the union and leadership then attended every briefing to discuss the goals of the project and listen to the concerns of line officers. Subsequently, various privacy concerns raised during these sessions were addressed in the department's final policy. The same process has been reported in several other departments, such as Mesa and Phoenix (Arizona) and Rialto (California).[19] However, research examining officer privacy concerns is rudimentary at best, and there is no research directly assessing how officers' privacy concerns affect their day-to-day activities.

Summary

A handful of studies have examined BWC citizen and officer privacy issues, but the results are mixed, without clear conclusions. Five studies surveyed citizens for their general perceptions on BWCs and privacy: two reported low levels of concern, and three reported moderate levels of concern. The results in these studies also varied depending on who was surveyed: the general population or citizens who had specifically come into contact with the police. Three studies examined BWCs and citizens' willingness to offer information to the police: one reported higher levels, one reported lower levels, and one showed no difference when BWCs were present. Only five studies have examined officer privacy in any depth, and all operationalized the issue differently. Much like the variation in the procedural justice studies reviewed in chapter 2, the mixed findings in this area may be explained by local context or methodological/operationalization issues. Clearly, more research is needed. Researchers should directly examine the impact of BWCs on levels of crime reporting for all different types of crimes. For instance, Cynthia Lum and colleagues suggest a study that compares "areas and officers with and without BWCs and the levels of 911 calls for service over time, or a test in which police dispatchers ask individuals when they call whether they would like officers to respond with or without BWCs activated."[20] Another possibility might involve a comparison of witnesses' testimony length and quality between BWC and non-BWC investigations.

Despite the lack of research in this area, privacy issues are a clear priority for police departments. Departments need to develop policies that protect citizen and officer privacy while still promoting transparency. One of the ways this balance can be struck is through the use of redaction technology—blurring images of faces or other identifiers prior to public release of videos. Considering recent advancements in video analytics, you might think this process would be relatively easy and accurate; you would be wrong. Not only is redaction technology incredibly difficult to implement (due to moving images, conversion difficulties, and quality control), but it also requires a considerable amount of staff resources (see Box 3.2). The contributions of additional staff can be difficult to budget at the beginning of a BWC program since the volume of public and media requests is unknown. In the next section, we discuss cost and resource requirements in more detail.

BOX 3.2

"State law regulating public records will determine the amount of staff time required to prepare video for release in response to public records requests. Identifying and copying video is the easy part; identifying and redacting sections of video and audio prohibited from release is time-consuming. We will be dependent upon improvements in video redaction technology to reduce this staff time drain."
—Gary Jenkins, Chief of Police, Pullman (Washington) Police Department (authors' interview)

Costs and Resource Requirements

An unavoidable reality is that BWCs cost money, and the costs go far beyond the initial investment in cameras and associated infrastructure. Agencies must maintain the technology and hire personnel to process videos. Early in the evolution of BWC programs, it was common for agencies to budget for cameras and servers but ignore continuous costs like video storage and personnel for program management (see Box 3.3). We have heard countless grumbles from police leadership about the difficulty anticipating just how many new personnel are required to support a BWC program. This is often because each department's infrastructure is idiosyncratic. For example, it is challenging to estimate exactly how much time it will take to categorize videos to interface with current records management systems (see Box 3.4) or to anticipate the likely volume of open-records requests (see Box 3.5).

BOX 3.3

"Many early adopters of BWCs focused on the cost of the cameras without considering the long-term costs of video storage and the personnel needed to maintain the program. It is now recognized that storage comprises the largest portion of a BWC budget, and staff time required for data management is proportional to the amount of data stored."

—Gary Jenkins, Chief of Police, Pullman (Washington) Police Department (authors' interview)

BOX 3.4

"Currently, officers must manually categorize videos with at least one of the fourteen different descriptive category options, assign an Incident Based Report (IBR) number, and title the video. If an officer spends an average of five minutes per video on these front-end data management steps multiplied by twelve videos a shift, an hour of the officer's time is lost to BWC data management per shift. This adds up to 120 hours department-wide every 24 hours, for a total of 43,800 hours a year dedicated to BWC data management rather than time on patrol.

Ideally, BWCs should be paired and integrated with in-car computer systems in a manner that would enable auto-population of Incident Based Report numbers and calls for service categories initiated by 911 dispatch. Having these two key video identifiers auto-populated for officers would greatly reduce the amount of time they spend on front-end data management of BWC videos and ultimately be a cost savings for police departments and their jurisdictions. Until this integration technology is developed and widely available, manual entry of IBR numbers and categories must be performed by officers at the cost of their departments and the communities they serve."

—Carolyn Naoroz, Body-Worn Camera Administrative Project Analyst, Richmond (Virginia) Police Department (authors' interview)

BOX 3.5

"Although not entirely unanticipated, the volume of 'open records' requests for BWC footage has been nearly overwhelming. Media requests and requests from defense attorneys and prosecutors and from local activists have greatly diminished the ability of the Open Records Section to respond promptly even with the addition of personnel."
—Edward A. Flynn, Chief (retired), Milwaukee Police Department (authors' interview)

Given the large cost and resource requirements of BWCs, it is surprising that there have been so few cost-benefit analyses. The Toronto Police Service found that the time required to investigate complaints against officers reduced if BWC footage was available, implying a useful cost savings.[21] Anthony Braga and colleagues conducted a more formal cost-benefit analysis with the Las Vegas Metropolitan Police Department (LVMPD). Given that LVMPD BWC officers average twenty-five complaints per one hundred officers annually, compared to eighty-four complaints per one hundred officers without BWCs, the cost savings associated with investigating complaints is significant. Using these calculations, Braga and colleagues estimated that "BWCs save over $6,200 in officer time spent investigating an average complaint, compared to complaint investigations for officers without BWCs."[22] While it is important that future research include cost-benefit analyses generally, specific agency costs should be investigated. For instance, there is no research on the cost savings associated with reduced officer misconduct or officer-involved shootings, improved investigations and prosecutions, and improved caliber of training systems. In the next section, we review the internal requirements associated with BWC implementation, specifically focusing on BWC policy and policy alignment.

Internal Requirements: BWC Policy

It has been said that technology does not reform organizations but rather organizations shape the use of the technology.[23] If so, they shape its use through policy and procedures. BWCs can benefit a police department in all the ways discussed in chapter 2, but they have no chance of succeeding if the technology is not used as intended. A well-formed, well-researched policy can help protect both the officer and department from critique and litigation. In this section, we review the research on key policy issues: officer activation, officer deactivation, citizen notification, officer review of BWC footage, and supervisor review of footage.

Again there is a lack of research in the area of BWC policy analysis. The notable exception is White and colleagues' policy analysis of over two hundred agencies that received US Department of Justice (DOJ) funding to implement BWC programs. They identified "common themes in BWC policies, with an eye toward identifying trends that could serve as a guide for law enforcement agencies nationwide."[24] We use this research as the primary source of evidence for this section.

BWC Assignment

A good BWC policy starts by identifying which officers in the department will be assigned a camera. All policies analyzed by White and colleagues delineate who will be given a BWC,[25] and it is standard practice to begin by deploying BWCs to officers assigned to patrol. Janne Gaub and colleagues note, "The focus on patrol is reasonable, as patrol officers represent the majority of a department's sworn personnel (typically 60–65%), and they are responsible for the majority of public contacts."[26] However, Gaub et al. also note that, as BWCs have become more integrated into police operations, an increasing number of departments are deploying BWCs to officers in nonpatrol functions, such as investigations, tactical units, and specialty assignments (anticrime, undercover, gang, and narcotics units).[27] Unfortunately, there are no available data on the number of police departments that have deployed BWCs to officers in nonpatrol assignments. Gaub and colleagues interviewed seventy-two officers assigned to seventeen different specialty units in two police departments, and results indicate that departments need to think carefully about the rollout of BWCs to such units: "Our study suggests that SUs [specialty units] present challenges for agencies in terms of policy and procedure. For units that work longer-than-average shifts, policies developed for general patrol may not translate well. Specific policy positions on activation, video-tagging, and downloading may have to be altered for SUs. For other units, such as those working with dignitaries or confidential informants, BWCs may be altogether inappropriate for their mission. For some SUs, then, our findings suggest that a completely different policy and program may be warranted."[28]

Officer Activation

A good BWC policy tells officers when cameras should be activated. Consider the following scenario: Two officers wearing BWCs are patrolling a popular strip of bars at 4:30 a.m. when they see a motorcycle driving erratically. They confront the driver, and moments later the motorcyclist ends up dead. The BWCs should have recorded the whole incident, but there was only one problem—the cameras were not turned on. This is exactly what happened on September 11, 2016, in Washington, DC.[29] The incident prompted demonstrations and reaction from numerous city officials, including the mayor. Instances such as this illustrate the importance of a clear BWC activation policy. White and colleagues report that departments vary substantially in the amount of discretion officers are given concerning camera activation.[30] Some departments mandate that officers record all citizen interactions, while others provide a list of incident types when recording is required. All departments in the White et al. study restrict recording certain types of situations (usually interactions involving an attorney, spouse, or confidential source or taking place in locker rooms). About three-quarters of policies allow officer discretion in activation, if mandatory and prohibited criteria are not in play.

Officer Deactivation

A BWC policy should also provide clear guidance on camera deactivation. In Sacramento (California), moments after police shot and killed Stephon Clarke on March 19, 2018, officers muted their BWCs. As in the Washington, DC, incident, there were demonstrations and public outcry. In response, the Sacramento Police Department amended its BWC policy to reflect that officers "shall not deactivate or mute their BWCs until the investigative or enforcement activity involving a member of the public has concluded." The policy still provides exceptions to this mandate, including "discussions with a doctor or nurse, when victims refuse to give a statement while being recorded or when the incident involves 'sensitive circumstances' such as sexual assault."[31]

White and colleagues report that over 80 percent of policies mandate deactivation after the conclusion of the event. However, the more recent trend is to avoid mandatory language and allow officers to use a certain amount of discretion in deactivation. As in Sacramento, many policies also specify circumstances when officers have discretion to deactivate. Discretionary deactivation clauses "address the need to protect persons (e.g., privacy of a crime victim), places (e.g., hospital locations) and information (e.g., tactical or operational discussions) during a police-citizen encounter."[32] As of 2017, almost all of the policies reviewed by White and colleagues include this discretionary language.[33]

Citizen Notification

Many of the purported benefits of BWCs are circumvented by citizens' lack of awareness. If citizens do not know they are being recorded, it is logical to assume that the civilizing effect of BWCs is not going to occur. In addition, public perceptions of police transparency and enhanced legitimacy are short-circuited. For these reasons, some police departments have mandatory citizen notification policies. White and colleagues find that about one-quarter of BWC policies have a mandatory statement on notification (e.g., "Member shall inform all individuals identifiably present as soon as reasonably practical, that their oral/video communications will be or have been intercepted and recorded").[34] A further 40 percent of policies recommend, but do not mandate, notification. There is an important caveat to add to this discussion. Researchers have shown that even when citizens are notified of BWCs, many do not subsequently recall the presence of a recording device.[35] Keep in mind that citizens who are recorded by police may be traumatized, angry, intoxicated, or mentally ill and in crisis. In plain terms, many citizens are not in a state of mind in which they can hear and understand an officer's notification of the BWC. Placement of the BWC may also have an impact on citizens' awareness. For example, a BWC mounted on an officer's sunglasses or hat may be more visible than a chest-mounted BWC (where it blends in with the rest of the officer's equipment). Officers could also wear a small placard or sign indicating to citizens that they are being recorded on a BWC. In order to guide police departments in this area, it will be useful if analysts conduct more research in the area of citizen notification.

Officer Review of BWC Footage

Officers' authority to review their own BWC footage is a controversial issue. Advocates of officer review state that BWC footage refreshes an officer's memory of an incident and increases the accuracy of reports and court testimony. Critics argue that BWC review can change an officer's memory and inhibit accurate reporting of what occurred. This debate is especially contentious in the wake of officer-involved shootings. We invited two experts in the area to weigh in on the debate in Box 3.6.

BOX 3.6

Argument against Pre-Report Review

"The desire to reduce criticism by allowing officers to review body-worn video footage before they complete use-of-force reports is understandable, but doing so will ultimately cause more problems than it solves. Adopting a 'pre-report review' policy decreases the accuracy of reports, risks diluting the legal standard, and courts public controversy.

Pre-report review decreases the accuracy of reports. In use-of-force cases, determining whether an officer acted lawfully and within policy requires understanding the officer's perceptions at the time. It is critical for a use-of-force report to accurately document an officer's contemporaneous perceptions. Allowing pre-report review, however, can supplant the officer's perspective with the camera's perspective. There is always the potential for conscious substitution, of course—officers choosing to include details from the video that they know they did not personally observe—but the bigger and more insidious risk comes from the nature of memory itself. Memory science teaches us that memories aren't fixed; they are subject to modifications that we are not consciously aware of. An officer who watches a video may very well have their perceptions change, their memories overwritten by information gleaned from the video. When that happens, the officer's report is not an accurate record of their contemporaneous perceptions.

Pre-report may change the legal standard. When use-of-force cases are litigated, the constitutional question is whether an officer's actions were objectively reasonable. As the Supreme Court wrote in *Graham v. Connor*, 'The "reasonableness" of a particular use of force must be judged from the perspective of a reasonable officer on the scene.' 490 U.S. 386, 396 (1989). This can be a very different perspective than the perspective of a camera on the scene. A camera, for example, sees both more and less than the human eye does. While the human eye has a fairly narrow band of focus (about two degrees of foveal vision), a camera can focus on just about anything that's in front of it. At the same time, a camera's field of view, which currently range from 68° to 143°, is narrower than that of the human eye, which ranges from 170° to 200°. Those differences mean that video footage simply cannot be an accurate representation of the officer's perceptions. Further, video footage is subject to misinterpretation because of 'deceptive intensity': the potential for viewers to overestimate the amount of speed and movement—and thus, the intensity of the action—in body-worn camera footage. Deceptive intensity can result from a confluence of where body-worn cameras are mounted, the way they move, and absence of the physiological and neurological processes by which we normally interpret movement, including the vestibulo-ocular reflex (the way our eyes move as our head moves), visual saccadic masking (the way our brains suppress visual information while our eyes are moving), and the lack of proprioception (the sense of where our body parts are). As a result, movements in video can appear far faster and more dramatic than they actually were. In short, while it can certainly provide valuable information, video footage does not accurately capture the perspective of the officer on the scene. Despite these differences, courts are more likely to review the reasonableness of a use of force from the perspective of the camera on the scene, rather than the perspective of an officer on the scene, if police agencies normalize pre-report review. After all, if police agencies and individual officers rely on video footage instead of officers' perceptions, they can hardly object to courts doing the same.

Pre-report review invites controversy. Police legitimacy suffers when the public perceives officers as benefiting from special protections that other community members do not enjoy. Imagine an apparently lawful civilian use of deadly force: say, a store owner who shoots a would-be armed robber. The store owner will, in all likelihood, not be treated like a criminal suspect. However, the store owner also will not be allowed to review security video footage before being interviewed and providing a statement. As with the store owner, it is not necessarily appropriate to treat an officer who uses force as a criminal suspect. However, allowing an officer to review video of the incident can create the appearance of preferential treatment, a perception that can seriously undermine public trust. Further, although advocates of pre-report review are understandably concerned about discrepancies between videos and officers' use-of-force reports creating doubts about individual incidents, pre-report review creates a bigger problem: individual discrepancies are explicable, but the complete absence of discrepancies across multiple cases is not. Inevitably, an academic conducting a study, a subject matter expert retained in litigation, or a Department of Justice investigation will compare hundreds or thousands of use-of-force reports to the underlying videos. When that happens, a finding that the reports match the events shown on video 100 percent of the time will be inherently suspicious, resulting in far more significant controversy and criticism than dealing with the entirely understandable discrepancies that can occur in any individual case.

Adopting pre-report review in an attempt to reduce or avoid criticism is shortsighted and will ultimately prove counterproductive. The better approach by far is for officers to write a use-of-force report based on their own recollections prior to watching any video. A reviewer should then assess the report, video, and other evidence; any points of inconsistency should be identified and, when possible, explained in the course of a review or investigation. This approach preserves the integrity of the report, is more faithful to the legal standard, and is ultimately better for police-community relations."
—Seth Stoughton, Associate Professor, University of South Carolina School of Law (authors' interview)

Argument in Favor of Pre-Report Review

"A police officer standing next to a motorist during a routine traffic stop suddenly hears gunshots coming from down the street. With his body-worn video camera activated, he runs toward the gunfire and sees a man shooting toward a house. The officer quickly draws his weapon and yells at the man to drop the gun. The man suddenly turns toward the officer and fires a handgun. The officer returns fire, striking the suspect, who then falls to the ground.

With his heart racing, the officer yells into his radio that he needs help and that a suspect is down. He cautiously approaches the man and sees a semiautomatic pistol lying next to him. The officer handcuffs the man as neighbors scream and police sirens swirl all around. The entire incident lasted fifteen seconds and has been recorded on the officer's body-worn video camera.

The officer is required by his department to write a complete report that accurately describes the precise details of what he saw, heard, and did before, during, and after the deadly encounter. He will be required to detail how many shots were fired, what the suspect looked like, what the suspect did, and why he chose to employ certain tactics and use deadly force.

The report will be used, in part, to determine what the officer's perceptions were at the time he used deadly force and to evaluate the tactical decisions and other actions he took during the incident. In addition, like most police reports, the officer may use the statement to refresh his recollection of the event prior to or during testimony in court.

Given its importance, should the officer be allowed to view his body-worn video footage before writing his report?

Every police agency in the nation allows officers to review interview notes, video and audio recordings, and other evidence before completing a report of an arrest, search, traffic collision, or other reported crime. The law also allows an officer, or any other witness, to review and use documents to ensure accurate testimony at trial. Most departments that have adopted body-worn video technology similarly allow officers to review their video before writing a report or providing a statement regarding a use of deadly force to ensure its completeness and accuracy.

This approach is based on the understanding that human memory is fallible and that recalling precise details of a traumatic and life-threatening situation is particularly difficult. Allowing officers to review their body-worn video enables accurate reporting by allowing them to refresh their recollections of the incident and allowing them to describe what occurred and why.

Critics of allowing officers to view video footage before writing their report argue that doing so reduces the accuracy of their reporting. They contend that watching the video may supplant the officer's memory of the event and that the best way to determine the officer's perceptions at the time is to interview them without any opportunity to refresh their memories. This argument is flawed for two important reasons.

First, simply asking the officer to recall the details of an intense, high-stress, life-and-death incident is not the same as asking the officer for what his perception was at the time. When someone describes what occurred in the past, he is not replaying the incident based on a fixed memory but instead is being tested to see what he can accurately recall of the incident. Thus, what the officer actually witnessed and what he is able to recall can be two entirely different questions.

Second, there is little or no reliable evidence that an officer's memory will be supplanted if he is allowed to view his video before writing a report. On the other hand, a large body of research has found that memories are highly susceptible to error because of the lapse of time or the introduction of false or erroneous information. Body-worn video provides evidence of what actually occurred, based on the officer's general perspective. Therefore, an officer is more likely to recall what he experienced by viewing the video recording of what actually transpired.

Inviting memory errors by prohibiting officers from reviewing body-worn video will also degrade the public's confidence in an investigation.

Imagine, for example, that the officer in the scenario above recalls that he first heard three gunshots, ran north, saw the suspect with the gun turn toward him and shoot two rounds, and the officer then returned fire with five shots. The video, however, reveals that only two shots were initially audible, the officer ran east (not north), and the suspect only fired one round at him. Most significantly, the officer returned fire with seven and not five rounds at the suspect.

These predictable inaccuracies and innocent errors will often be construed as false statements and will call into question the veracity of the officer's report. Therefore, prohibiting an officer from reviewing body-worn video footage will inevitably lead to less accurate recollections of what the officer witnessed during the encounter.

Allowing officers to review video footage captured by their body-worn cameras is consistent with procedures in place for many decades, and the arguments to change the practice are not supported by reliable evidence. Current practices enable increased accuracy of reports by refreshing the recollections of officers and avoid undermining the integrity of investigations through common memory errors and predictable inconsistencies."

—Arif Alikhan, Director, Office of Constitutional Policing and Policy, Los Angeles Police Department (authors' interview)

Despite the contentious nature of this issue, White and colleagues show that nearly all agencies allow officer review of BWC footage for routine report writing and court preparation (e.g., "Officers assigned a BWC are encouraged to review BWC media prior to completing any investigative reports").[36] Allowing unfettered officer review during an administrative investigation following a critical incident such as a complaint against an officer or use of force is far less prevalent. Only approximately one-quarter of departments allow officers to have unrestricted access to the BWC footage in these circumstances.[37] Most departments allow officers to review footage as long as certain stipulations are met, such as having a union representative or member of the command staff present. And under 10 percent of departments restrict officer access to BWC footage completely following a critical incident, such as an officer-involved shooting.[38] The vast majority of federally funded agencies allow their officers to view the video of a shooting first, before making a statement.

Supervisor Review of BWCs

The White et al. policy review identified three types of supervisor review of subordinate officers' BWC footage: (1) administrative review, (2) compliance review, and (3) performance review.[39] Over 95 percent of all DOJ-funded agencies allow first-line supervisors to review BWC footage as part of an administrative review, such as use-of-force or complaint investigations. The number stays about the same for compliance review, with over 90 percent of department policies allowing supervisor review to ensure compliance with BWC policy and procedures (e.g., auditing for activation compliance). The most contentious type of supervisory BWC viewing involves performance review. However, over 90 percent of 2016 and 2017 DOJ-funded departments allow supervisors to review line officers' BWC footage for this purpose.[40] A clear and effective supervisory review policy and auditing system should help departments achieve their stated BWC program goals, including increased transparency, accountability, and legitimacy (see Box 3.7). Additionally, BWCs can also serve as a useful training tool, as supervisors can view footage to identify areas where officers need additional coaching or instruction. Nearly all of the policies reviewed by White and colleagues allow BWC footage to be used for training purposes.[41]

BOX 3.7

"It isn't practical for a department (unless very small) to look at every video. No one has the resources to do that. However, the department should be looking constantly at broad segments in an organized, documented fashion. To be clear, this isn't looking at individual officer performance. Departments have first line supervision and command to handle those issues, as well as internal affairs processes. One officer's failures do not equate to widespread department failure. However, if the failure is consistent across the department then it must be corrected immediately. Positive behaviors must also be identified and reinforced in department processes."
—Dan Zehnder, Captain (retired), Las Vegas Metropolitan Police Department, and President, Principis Group (author's interview)

Summary

In this section, we emphasized the importance of a strong BWC policy but also explored how policies are different and suggest that they may need to be tailored to the local context. One size does not fit all. Policies will continue to evolve as BWC technology develops and as states weigh in with policy requirements and/or laws. Technology, such as facial recognition analysis, speech-to-text capabilities, and wireless upload of digital footage, will inevitably continue to evolve, and departments need to remain vigilant in maintaining their policies.[42]

Impact on Officer Activity

Two concerns have emerged regarding the potential impact of BWCs on police officer activity. The first concern is that deployment of BWCs, as a form of surveillance that allows for internal (by supervisors) and external (public) scrutiny of officer behavior, may lead to reduced activity, or what is termed "depolicing." A second concern centers on the impact of BWCs on officer discretion; more specifically, officers will *increase* their formal activity (stops, citations, arrests, etc.) rather than handling encounters informally (e.g., warnings). The hypothesis that supports this position is that officers may reduce use of discretion to avoid postincident questioning from supervisors who challenge the decision to resolve an encounter informally (in other words, "why didn't you arrest?"). Each of these concerns is described in greater detail in the following subsections, followed by a review of the existing research on BWCs and officer activity.

BWCs and the Potential for Depolicing

There is a contentious debate over whether heightened public scrutiny of police since 2014 has led to "depolicing," or an intentional reduction in police officer activity.[43] For example, former FBI director James Comey repeatedly linked the intense focus on police with less aggressive police tactics, suggesting that the "viral video effect blunts police work" (see Text Box 3.8).[44] Heather MacDonald has asserted that public scrutiny of police led to increases in violent crime and attacks on police officers via a "Ferguson effect."[45] Review of the body of research examining the "Ferguson effect" exceeds the scope of this book,[46] but there is some evidence to suggest that officer activity levels may have changed post-Ferguson. For example, John Shjarback and colleagues found that Missouri police agencies conducted sixty-seven thousand fewer traffic stops in 2015 compared to 2014, with the biggest declines observed in predominantly African American municipalities.[47] There is also psychological research demonstrating that enhanced surveillance of employees can negatively affect employee motivation and even lead to counterproductive workplace behaviors.[48]

BOX 3.8

"Nobody says it on the record, nobody says it in public, but police and elected officials are quietly saying it to themselves. And they're saying it to me, and I'm going to say it to you. And it is the one explanation that does explain the calendar and the map and that makes the most sense to me. Maybe something in policing has changed. In today's YouTube world, are officers reluctant to get out of their cars and do the work that controls violent crime? Are officers answering 911 calls but avoiding the informal contact that keeps bad guys from standing around, especially with guns?"
—Former FBI Director James Comey, "Law Enforcement and the Communities We Serve," October 23, 2015

The question is whether BWCs could contribute to depolicing. Some critics have argued that BWCs, as a form of surveillance, are part of this larger movement to publicly scrutinize police. There is certainly some merit to this claim; advocacy groups support BWCs primarily because of their potential to monitor police officer behavior.[49] Barak Ariel and colleagues speculate on this question by suggesting that the effects of BWCs on officer behavior are determined by a delicate balance between officer discretion and deterrence.[50] BWCs have a deterrent effect on officer misuse of force in that cameras provide surveillance that increases the likelihood of sanctions. Ariel and colleagues go on to argue that optimal deterrence can be achieved with strong controls on discretion, but when a department applies an approach that is too heavy-handed, "'over-deterrence' and even 'inertia' are possible, which are manifested in police withdrawal"[51]—in other words, depolicing.

BWCs and Officer Discretion

The second concern about BWCs is that the technology may negatively affect officers' use of discretion. Discretion is a central and appropriate feature of the police role.[52] Officers often have legal authority to take formal action—issue a citation, make an arrest, and so on—and they choose not to do so. Instead, they handle the encounter informally through a warning, referral, or other resolution that does not involve a formal sanction. As far back as 1967, the President's Commission on Law Enforcement and the Administration of Justice recognized, "police should openly acknowledge that, quite properly, they do not arrest all, or even most, offenders they know of."[53] Critics of BWCs have argued that the cameras may serve to restrict officers' appropriate use of discretion, either because of concerns that their decisions will be second-guessed later by supervisors or because the department has become too heavy-handed in its efforts to control officer discretion.[54] Survey research with police officers provides some support for this concern. For example, Gaub et al. surveyed officers from three police departments, and post-BWC deployment, most officers agreed or strongly agreed that BWCs make them feel like they have less discretion (Phoenix, 82.4 percent; Spokane, 50.5 percent; and Tempe, 56.3 percent).[55]

Research Examining BWCs and Officer Activity

Thirteen studies have considered the impact of BWCs on specific types of officer activity: arrests, citations, and proactive policing. Table 3.1 shows that the findings are quite mixed. As in earlier tables, each entry in table 3.1 includes basic information about the study: the agency, the state, the researchers, the year of the publication, and the rigor of the study as determined by its rating on the Maryland Scale of Scientific Methods (SMS).[56] The next column provides a visual indicator of the study's summary findings: a down arrow for a decline in arrests, citations, or proactivity (such as traffic stops); an up arrow for an increase; and a null sign for no statistical or substantive change. A solid arrow indicates that the change is statistically significant (p < .05). The final column illustrates the sample size per group.

TABLE 3.1. Officer Activity Research

Agency	Location	Authors	Year	Rigor	Finding	Sample size
Anaheim PD	California	McClure et al.	2017	☐☐☐☐☐	▼ Arrests	◇
DC Met PD	DC	Yokum et al.	2017	☐☐☐☐☐	⊘ Arrests	◇◇◇◇◇◇
Denver PD	Colorado	Ariel	2016	☐☐☐	▼ Arrests	◇◇◇◇◇
Hallandale Beach PD	Florida	Headley et al.	2017	☐☐☐☐	▼ Arrests ▲ Proactivity △ Citations	◇◇
Las Vegas Metro PD	Nevada	Braga et al.	2018	☐☐☐☐☐	▼ Arrests + citations ⊘ Proactivity	◇◇◇◇◇
London Metro PD	England	Grossmith et al.	2015	☐☐☐☐☐	⊘ Arrests	◇◇◇◇◇◇
Mesa PD	Arizona	Ready and Young	2015	☐☐☐	▼ Arrests ▲ Citations	◇◇◇
Milwaukee PD	Wisconsin	Peterson et al.	2018	☐☐☐☐☐	▼ Stops ⊘ Arrests	◇◇◇◇◇
Phoenix PD	Arizona	Hedberg et al. Katz et al.	2017 2014	☐☐☐☐	⊘ Arrests ▲ Arrests	◇◇◇
Plymouth Constabulary	England	Goodall	2007	☐☐	△ Arrests	◇◇◇◇◇
Spokane PD	Washington	Wallace et al.	2018	☐☐☐☐☐	⊘ Arrests + ▲ Proactivity	◇◇◇◇
Toronto PS	Canada	Toronto PS	2016	☐☐☐	△ Arrests ▽ Citations	◇◇◇◇

☐ Level 1	▲ significant increase	◇ < 25 per group
☐☐ Level 2	△ increase	◇◇ 25–49 per group
☐☐☐ Level 3	▼ significant decrease	◇◇◇ 50–74 per group
☐☐☐☐ Level 4	▽ decrease	◇◇◇◇ 75–99 per group
☐☐☐☐☐ Level 5	⊘ null	◇◇◇◇◇ 100–499 per group
		◇◇◇◇◇◇ > 500 per group

Charles Katz and colleagues conducted a quasi-experiment in Phoenix and found that BWC-assigned officers increased their arrest activity by more than 40 percent following camera deployment.[57] However, using a more sophisticated analytic technique controlling for activation, Eric Hedberg and colleagues found no measurable difference in arrests between BWC and non-BWC groups.[58] This emphasizes the importance of taking contamination and activation into account. Justin Ready and Jacob Young examined the impact of BWCs on officer activity in Mesa (Arizona), and they concluded, "At the outset of the study, a major concern among the commanding officers was that body-worn cameras might cause officers to be less proactive or more reluctant to initiate contacts with citizens, instead focusing most of their time on dispatched calls. We found this not to be the case. On the contrary, camera officers actually initiated significantly more contacts with citizens than comparison officers."[59] Braga et al. also reported increases in arrests and citations among BWC officers in Las Vegas but found no change in police proactivity.[60] Alternatively, multiple studies and Ready and Young all found that officers with BWCs made significantly fewer arrests.[61] Grossmith et al. reported no impact on "the number or type of stop and searches," self-reported activity, or arrest decisions.[62] David Yokum and colleagues, in their RCT with the Washington, DC, Metropolitan Police, found a similar null effect on level of arrests.[63]

Several studies have concluded that the impact of BWCs on officer activity is nuanced and complex. Ready and Young found that, despite having increased citizen contacts, BWC officers made fewer arrests but issued more citations, which the authors attributed to officers' concerns about supervisory review of their decisions.[64] Bryce Peterson et al. reported similarly complex findings in Milwaukee: "First, officers wearing BWCs conducted significantly fewer subject stops than officers without cameras. However, patterns of arrests and traffics stops were similar across the two groups. This indicates that officers equipped with a BWC became more selective in who they approached and stopped during their patrol activities, but BWCs may have had no effect on whether officers stopped a vehicle or made an arrest."[65] Danielle Wallace and colleagues explored the potential for BWCs to generate depolicing through a hypothesized "camera-induced passivity."[66] More specifically, they tested the impact of BWCs in Spokane on four different measures of officer activity: self-initiated activity, arrests, response time, and time on scene. They found no evidence of depolicing: BWCs had no impact on arrests, response time, or time on scene. In fact, BWC officers actually increased their self-initiated activity, directly refuting the depolicing thesis.[67]

Summary

A handful of studies have examined the impact of BWCs on officer activity, and the results are quite mixed. For example, thirteen studies have tested the impact of BWCs on arrests: four reported an increase,[68] four reported a decrease,[69] and five reported no effect.[70] Four studies examine the impact on citations: three reported an increase,[71] and one reported a decrease.[72] Much like the variation in studies examining force and complaints, the mixed findings in this area may also be explained by local context, planning and implementation, or other factors. Braga et al. raise an important concern about the consequences of increased formal activity: "It is possible that increased enforcement activity associated with BWCs might enhance legitimacy by improving police effectiveness in controlling crime and their capacity to hold offenders accountable. . . . Alternatively, increased enforcement activity could undermine police legitimacy if citizens view heightened arrests and citations as harmful to their communities."[73] Clearly, more research would provide a deeper understanding of the potential for BWCs to affect officers' activity levels, either through depolicing or by inhibiting their appropriate use of discretion.

External Stakeholder Commitment and Coordination

BWC programs are not implemented in a vacuum: several different stakeholder agencies can impact internal success of the technology. For example, the reluctance of a police union to support BWCs could delay implementation or create morale issues with rank-and-file officers, while ignoring city leaders' concerns about the technology could lead to budgetary problems in the future. The reverse is also true: implementation of BWCs can influence local institutions outside the police department. For instance, the prosecutor's office may require additional resources to review BWC footage, and other first responders such as nearby police departments and fire and rescue will need to prepare for the likelihood that they will be recorded at the scene of an accident. For these reasons, early and consistent engagement with police unions, neighboring police departments, prosecutors and public defenders, courts, city leaders, fire and rescue, and citizen and advocacy groups is important when implementing a BWC program (see Box 3.9). In this section, we discuss how external stakeholders are both affected by and influence the implementation of BWCs.

BOX 3.9

"As I look back several years after starting this project, I can say without a doubt that taking the time to adequately plan for the implementation of digital evidence and body-worn cameras in our organization was the best decision we made. Taking the time to set goals, identify timelines, pursue funding, communicate with the public, involve a robust group of internal and external stakeholders to actually implement the project, and work with a research partner *before* a camera was ever put on an officer in the field allowed us to effectively implement our BWC program without resistance or delay."
—Brenda Buren, Assistant Chief/Director, Tempe (Arizona) Police Department (authors' interview)

Police Unions

Union buy-in is essential for a successful BWC program, as unions have the ability to either facilitate or hinder rates of officer acceptance; but getting police unions on board is sometimes a difficult task. In fact, unionized agencies are significantly less likely to adopt BWCs.[74] Some associations argue that BWCs fundamentally change working conditions, necessitating a new union contract.[75] In a particularly strong stance against the technology, the Boston (Massachusetts) police union sued the Boston Police Department and sought an injunction to halt the implementation of the cameras. The union cited the involuntary nature of the proposed pilot program and research results reporting that officers were more likely to be assaulted if wearing BWCs.[76] In Hallandale Beach (Florida), the union initially opposed BWCs on the basis that they would lead to depolicing and inhibit officers from undertaking their normal duties.[77] And in Las Vegas, the union contract made the BWC pilot project especially difficult, as the LVMPD could not mandate its officers to wear the cameras.[78] To avoid many of these issues and get the union on board, it is important for line officers and the union to be involved in the BWC planning process from the very beginning. The union is much more likely to trust leadership and support a BWC program if it is given a voice, allowed to express concerns, and given decision-making power at the start of the planning process (see Box 3.10).[79]

BOX 3.10

"Prior to body-worn cameras being deployed on first responders with the Phoenix Police Department, the technology was widely panned by internal detractors as nothing more than a means for supervisors to spy on officers. Some, to include the labor organization representing our officers, asserted that the cameras were a tool for management to go on thinly veiled 'fishing expeditions' designed to capture policy violations and administer discipline absent any formal citizen complaint. Our officers and their union quickly learned that the presence of the technology benefited the camera wearer far more often than not, particularly during controversial use-of-force incidents and other contentious interactions with the public."
—Michael J. Kurtenbach, Executive Assistant Chief, Phoenix Police Department (authors' interview)

Nearby Law Enforcement Agencies

When one police department adopts BWCs, it can affect neighboring law enforcement agencies in both positive and negative ways. We have worked with agencies that have implemented BWCs and then shared policy and procedure templates with other departments near and far. We also know of small agencies that have partnered to share costs for storage. The most common *contagious* benefit of a BWC program is the creation of local working groups and informal communication networks. The Bureau of Justice Assistance BWC Training and Technical Assistance (TTA) funds regional meetings where local departments that are thinking about or currently implementing BWCs can discuss issues and offer advice to one another. These meetings also provide a forum to discuss specific issues with the technology and its providers. But not all of the effects felt by neighboring agencies are positive. Once a police department adopts the technology, nearby departments might feel pressure from their city council and the public to implement BWCs, often regardless of whether there is a pressing need. This can lead to hastily implemented policies and infrastructure.

Prosecutors and Public Defenders

Next to the police department, prosecutors and public defenders are impacted most substantially by a BWC program. In jurisdictions where police have deployed BWCs, most criminal cases now come with BWC footage. These offices will need to develop their own policies and procedures for storing, processing, and utilizing the data, and new personnel and technology may be required. Therefore, they will probably need to do their own research and budget for the BWC program. To further complicate matters, prosecutors outside the local jurisdiction may have different data-management systems, and they may need to find a technological workaround in order to view and store the footage. Natalie Todak and colleagues conducted focus groups and interviews with stakeholders, including prosecutors and public defenders. These stakeholders reported significant concerns about the resource burden of video evidence. For example, one public defender reported that an extra four to ten hours of work will probably be required on a case when

BWC footage is present.[80] Prosecutors stated that setting up protocols for receiving and processing BWC evidence from the police could cause tension between the agencies.[81] For each of these reasons, it is important for police departments to engage with both offices early and often in the BWC adoption process (see Box 3.11).

BOX 3.11

"The police department here has been very kind and considerate in the way that they're rolling this out, as opposed to other jurisdictions that I've heard about who—the police department just kind of went 'Oh crap we need these on them' and then prosecuting offices suddenly had this large amount of video data where there's no system in place, there's no policies in place, and there are no resources to view them."
—city prosecutor, quoted in Todak, Gaub, and White, "Importance of External Stakeholders"

However, BWCs also benefit prosecutors and public defenders. Video evidence can help in cases where an officer's observations are the only way to determine probable cause.[82] Video footage can also inspire better compliance with procedures for gathering evidence. Todak and colleagues report that public defenders were hopeful that BWCs would protect defendants' rights, and prosecutors said it helps them in cases where victims or witnesses later recant their story (e.g., domestic violence).[83]

Courts

By the time BWC evidence makes it into the courts, most of the workload and technology issues have been resolved by police and prosecutors. In fact, judges acknowledge that BWCs might actually reduce their workload due to increased negotiations or plea bargains on the strength of video evidence.[84] However, the introduction of BWC evidence still changes the courtroom landscape. Judges will need to better understand the impact that BWCs have on public expectations of evidence. Do jurors presume high-quality video evidence in every case? And will its absence reduce the likelihood of a conviction? Judges need to educate themselves on the limitations of BWCs and make juries aware of these limits.

City Leaders

The costs and benefits of BWCs do not end in the courtroom; they extend into the larger community. The technology provides objective data on community problems and could potentially improve police-community relations through increased transparency, accountability, and legitimacy. We do not know of any city councils that would not be happy about this prospect. Despite city leaders being responsible for funding BWC programs, politicians are often the least informed about the technology. Police departments need to engage city leaders early in the BWC implementation process to communicate program goals and ensure that funding exists to maintain the technology.

Fire, Rescue, and Mental Health Teams

If a police department implements a BWC program, fire, rescue, and mental health teams in the local area will inevitably find themselves on camera. These agencies will have to be informed about when and where cameras will be operating in order to develop their own policies and training regarding BWCs. For instance, if a mental health team is meeting with a citizen in distress and asking about sensitive and private health-care matters, how does the team deal with an officer wearing a BWC within eye- or earshot? If video does capture confidential health-care information, what is the storage and redaction process for this footage? All agencies involved need to develop policy and procedures that can coexist and still protect a citizen's privacy. Because this policy landscape can become complicated very quickly, it is important that early drafts of policies from all groups be circulated preimplementation.

Citizens and Advocacy Groups

Last but certainly not least, police departments need to engage citizens and advocacy groups prior to implementing BWCs. As we mentioned at the beginning of this chapter, BWCs have the potential to infringe on citizens' privacy in many ways. They record sensitive information at a particular time when a citizen is often experiencing a low point, as a crime suspect or victim or as someone experiencing some sort of personal crisis. The public release of this information could be emotionally damaging or even dangerous. It is important to hear about privacy concerns directly from community members themselves. It is also important for the police to articulate their motives and vision of success for a BWC program. This will strengthen the possibility that BWCs could improve strained relationships between the community and police. An especially vigilant department will also run its policies by advocacy groups, such as the National Association for the Advancement of Colored People (NAACP) and ACLU. These groups will help ensure that the department balances the privacy of its citizens with transparency and increased evidentiary benefits.

Conclusion

In this chapter, we have discussed the challenges and limitations of BWCs. Even though there are many issues involved in implementing this technology, we do not feel these challenges are insurmountable. In fact, with some good planning and a sound knowledge of the research, police departments should be able to avoid most of the pitfalls. Our hope is that after reading chapters 2 and 3, the reader comes away with the view that not all police departments will reap the same benefits of BWCs. This is because, put simply, not all agencies start in the same place. Organizational culture and local community context affect the benefits of any technology. In the chapter 4, we elaborate on how departments resolve ongoing questions surrounding BWCs and answer the big question: will BWCs continue to spread and positively affect the policing world?

4

Understanding Body-Worn Camera Adoption

Past, Present, and Future

The rapid and widespread diffusion of police BWCs over the past few years is extraordinary, especially given the cost of the technology (financial and otherwise) and the complexity of issues involved. Quite simply, the challenges described in chapter 3 must appear overwhelming to the police chief just getting starting with this technology. Yet thousands of police departments have deployed BWCs. The BWC phenomenon raises interesting questions about the processes by which police departments adopt new technology, the manner in which initial concerns or questions over that technology are overcome, the progression that occurs over time to "normalize" use of that technology, and how success of the technology is measured. In the case of BWCs, four specific questions come to mind:

1. Why have BWCs spread so rapidly?
2. How have police departments resolved the ongoing questions about BWCs with their officers and their constituents?
3. Have BWCs achieved their desired effect?
4. Will BWCs continue to diffuse in policing?

In this chapter we try to make sense of BWC adoption by exploring these questions. In order to do so, we apply two theoretical frameworks to understand camera adoption: the diffusion of innovation and evidence-based policing frameworks. Each framework provides a lens to examine the how and why of BWC adoption in policing. And just as important, each framework provides a foundation to consider the prospects for continued diffusion in the years to come. The takeaway from both frameworks is a more thorough understanding of what has transpired over the past several years, as well as what is likely to occur in the future. Before delving into these frameworks, a quick review of the rise of BWCs in policing is warranted.

The Emergence of BWCs in Policing

The adoption of police BWCs has followed an uneven path. A handful of Canadian and European police departments began testing them in the early 2000s, and some US departments had deployed them as early as 2009.[1] According to a Bureau of Justice Statistics survey of law enforcement agencies in the United States, roughly one-third of respondents had some form of BWC deployment as of 2013, though most were limited programs or pilot studies.[2] In effect, there was a low and slow burning interest in the technology through early 2014.

Everything changed after the summer of 2014. The deaths of Michael Brown, Eric Garner, Tamir Race, and others placed tremendous scrutiny on police, led to riots and disorder in some cities (Baltimore, Ferguson), and generated national calls for police reform. Police BWCs drew significant attention during this time as a tool that could address some of the underlying problems that police and communities (especially communities of color) were experiencing. Advocates of the technology made bold statements about the impact of BWCs. Whether as a show of transparency, a way to hold officers accountable, or a way to enhance legitimacy, police departments across the United States quickly moved to roll out BWC programs. The federal government supported BWC adoption through both financial and technical assistance. Recall that just four months after Michael Brown was killed in Ferguson, Missouri, President Obama gave a speech at the White House where he pledged $75 million for the deployment of fifty thousand BWCs across the country. At a time when there were only a handful of evaluations (less than five) of the technology, this pledge represented a remarkable federal commitment to BWCs. The White House was essentially going all in with body-worn cameras.

Over the next four years, thousands of police departments across the United States adopted BWCs. Currently, it is unknown exactly how many departments have a BWC program. The Major City Chiefs and Major County Sheriffs Associations surveyed their membership in 2015, and nearly all indicated they were planning or had already implemented a BWC program: "only 5% of respondents said they either did not intend to implement a BWC program, or had completed a pilot but chose not to proceed."[3] The Bureau of Justice Statistics added BWC questions to its 2016 Law Enforcement Management and Administrative Statistics (LEMAS) survey, which is a national survey of police departments in the United States administered every three to five years.[4] Those results were released in fall 2018 and represent the most accurate estimate of BWC diffusion to date. Just under half (47 percent) of law enforcement agencies have deployed BWCs, including 80 percent of large agencies (more than five hundred sworn officers).[5] Of course, those results do not account for agencies that have deployed BWCs after 2016. That rate of adoption is striking. Now to the how and why questions: we start with the diffusion of innovation framework.

The Diffusion of Innovations Framework

Diffusion of innovation refers to the spread of an idea, information, tool, or practice from a source to a larger group.[6] Whether an innovation spreads, as well as how quickly it spreads, is determined by a number of factors. Does the innovation have value? Does it also have negative consequences? Are those consequences or risks the same for all adopters? The diffusion of innovation framework offers a lens for understanding how and why a technology spreads. Moreover, it can be used to make projections about the continued diffusion of an innovation (or not). The diffusion of innovation framework can be traced back to Bryce Ryan and Neal Gross's 1943 study of hybrid seed corn, and it has been used in

TABLE 4.1. The Diffusion of Innovation Framework

Innovation characteristics	Innovator characteristics	Environmental characteristics
Private and public consequences	Societal entity/social networks	Geographic/political conditions
Costs	Familiarity	Culture
Benefits	Status characteristics	

nearly four thousand studies since then. Barbara Wejnert extended the theory by creating a single conceptual framework that includes three different sets of factors that can influence diffusion: characteristics of the innovation (public and private consequences; costs and benefits), the innovators (societal entity/networks, familiarity, status and personal characteristics), and the environment (geographic and political conditions, societal culture).[7] Table 4.1 provides an overview of factors that make up the diffusion of innovation framework.

Wejnert's extension fits well with the diffusion of innovation in policing.[8] David Weisburd et al. applied the framework to consider the diffusion of CompStat,[9] and David Klinger expounded on its relevance for both CompStat and SWAT teams in US policing.[10] Michael White used the framework to examine the rapid diffusion of the TASER less-lethal device.[11] We employ the diffusion of innovation framework here to answer three of the aforementioned questions about police BWCs: Why have they spread so rapidly? How have departments resolved questions about their use? Will they continue to diffuse in policing? Through the diffusion of innovation lens, the widespread and rapid diffusion of BWCs will appear as a natural, rational development in policing.

Characteristics of the Innovation

The diffusion framework highlights two key issues associated with characteristics of the innovation (BWCs): the public and private consequences of its use; and the costs and benefits associated with its adoption. The consequences component of the framework addresses who is affected by its adoption, and it sets the stage for the discussion of costs and benefits.

PUBLIC AND PRIVATE CONSEQUENCES

The consequences of an innovation both for those who adopt it (private entities such as the police) and for others who might be affected by it (public entities or the community) will strongly influence a technology's diffusion pattern.[12] The consequences of BWCs for police (the innovators) are widespread, ranging from direct financial costs for purchasing the technology and training officers in its use to the implications of their use during police-citizen encounters. Much of this book is devoted to review and analysis of those consequences, both positive and negative (see chapters 2 and 3). The consequences of BWCs for police are linked to the goals a department wants to achieve through adoption of the technology, most commonly transparency with the community, evidentiary value, enhanced police legitimacy, greater civility during police-citizen encounters, and improved officer accountability. These are vitally important goals that go directly to the core of the police mission.

BWCs also have consequences that extend beyond the innovators (police) to the community and numerous other entities, most notably those downstream in the criminal justice system. In terms of the community, the potential for BWCs to demonstrate transparency and to enhance perceptions of police legitimacy (or at least public satisfaction) has clear consequences for citizens. Moreover, citizens are directly affected by BWCs, as they are recorded on the cameras during their interactions with police. In many cases, the BWC may capture citizens on the worst day of their lives. They may have experienced a trauma or victimization. They or a loved one may be intoxicated or mentally ill and in crisis. They may be angry, upset, or scared. The BWC memorializes that moment. Natalie Todak et al. interviewed numerous external stakeholders about BWCs, and a victim advocate poignantly highlighted the consequences of BWCs for victims: "We had somebody request every moment of footage from a body-worn camera. That's terrifying as a victim. This is your most vulnerable moment. . . . If someone is left in an alley or sidewalk or park, and a patrol officer gets the call, runs to the scene, is that person [officer] going to know whether to turn on their camera or remember to turn it off? Is this footage of them [victims] in a state of undress or disrepair or trauma, . . . [and] how accessible is that to the public?"[13]

The deployment of police BWCs has consequences for other local institutions such as the fire department, rescue/emergency medical services (EMS), mental health providers, hospitals, city government, local businesses, and schools. EMS and firefighters often respond to calls involving the police, and their actions will now also be captured on the BWC. The recording of patients in hospitals and students in schools represents privacy challenges that need to be addressed by police. And the resource consequences of BWC footage for downstream criminal justice actors (e.g., prosecutors, defense) are significant, as illustrated by Todak et al.:

> Some of the complaints I'm fielding already from our paralegal: . . . "I spent half a day or a full day just trying to sort through all these body camera videos." And this is just the initial roll out. . . . If you start adding to this exponentially where you have more and more of these officers with [BWCs], . . . who's going to be responsible for doing that? It doesn't come with a flag saying "Here's the important thing right here," this 10 minutes of 2 hours of a camera rolling. (Prosecutor)
>
> Interviewee 1: I would say that that's one of the most time consuming things that we do is watching video, everybody can agree with that.
>
> Interviewee 2: I have four that I need to watch right now!
>
> Interviewee 3: If the body cam's there, I'm looking at probably anywhere between an extra 4–10 hours working on a case, no matter what. (Public Defender Investigators)[14]

Clearly, BWCs have both private and public consequences. The costs and benefits of those consequences represent the second feature of an innovation that impacts diffusion.

BENEFITS

Chapter 2 is devoted to a full review of the evidence on the perceived benefits of BWCs, and quite clearly the research base supports a number of those benefits. The most commonly cited benefit of BWCs involves decreased rates of use of force by officers and citizen complaints against officers, presumably because of a civilizing effect generated by the camera's presence (through deterrence or some other mechanism). The BWC outcomes directories created by White and colleagues succinctly review the evidence on these benefits: twenty of twenty-six studies have reported a notable decline in complaints against officers following BWC deployment;[15] eleven of nineteen studies have reported a notable decline in use of force after BWC deployment.[16] Though not universal, the weight of the evidence regarding the effect of BWCs on citizen complaints and use of force is persuasive.

Several studies have also highlighted the evidentiary value of BWCs, particularly for the prosecution of domestic violence cases.[17] Scottish researchers found that BWC cases were 70–80 percent more likely to end in guilty plea.[18] Charles Katz et al. reported that BWC officers in Phoenix who received a complaint were significantly more likely to have that complaint unsubstantiated upon investigation.[19] Anthony Braga et al. conducted the first rigorous cost-benefit analysis of BWCs and concluded the Las Vegas Metropolitan Police Department program generated a cost savings of over $4 million per year.[20]

The arguments in favor of enhanced transparency and accountability are equally persuasive, though the empirical evidence is less robust. The American Civil Liberties Union (ACLU) notes, "Although we at the ACLU generally take a dim view of the proliferation of surveillance cameras in American life, police on-body cameras are different because of their potential to serve as a check against the abuse of power by police officers."[21] Chris Dunn and Donna Lieberman have highlighted the value of cameras for shedding light on high-profile citizen deaths, noting that the deaths of Eric Garner, Tamir Rice, and Walter Scott "have exploded into national controversies for the simple reason that they were caught on video."[22] Another important potential benefit of BWCs is that the cameras may enhance citizens' perceptions of police legitimacy. In one of the few studies to date to test this claim, White and colleagues identified an intriguing connection between citizens' awareness of the BWC during a police encounter and increased perceptions of procedural justice, "providing a preliminary piece of evidence that BWCs may be able to deliver on the claim the technology can enhance police legitimacy."[23]

COSTS

Chapter 3 details the evidence on the costs of BWCs, ranging from the significant financial and resource commitment required to external stakeholder engagement and weighty issues involving citizen and officer privacy. Certainly, the financial commitment required to deploy BWCs is considerable. The Denver Police Department reported their cost for eight hundred cameras and associated storage at more than $6 million.[24] As part of the cost-benefit analysis in Las Vegas, Braga et al. estimated the program cost at $1,097 per user per year, for a total annual cost of $891,390.[25] After BWC deployment, agencies must dedicate human resources to review and redact BWC footage for public records requests, provide hardware and software technical assistance to officers, audit metadata to assess proper use by officers (e.g., activation compliance), and deliver other system maintenance and assistance as needed. One chief reported how BWCs compete with other priorities for limited resources: "[One challenge of BWCs is the] financial competition for other needs I as chief see as a priority. Crime rate is low, public trust is acceptable, and there isn't a critical need. However, the politicians would like to see the BWC program implemented."[26]

BWCs may also have unintended consequences or costs. Some people have suggested that the presence of a BWC may aggravate citizens and increase the likelihood that they will resist or act violently toward officers. Barak Ariel and colleagues reported that BWC officers were more likely to be assaulted by citizens than were non-BWC officers.[27] However, other research has found no effect of BWCs on officer assaults and injuries.[28] Available research does show concerning trends in several policy-related areas. For example, studies show that most citizens are not aware that they are being recorded by a BWC, thereby short-circuiting any potential for a civilizing effect on citizen behavior.[29] Concerns about activation compliance (i.e., not activating the BWC) have also emerged, both generally and in the aftermath of officer-involved shootings that should have been recorded but were not (see chapter 5).[30]

Alternatively, the evidence on many of the other challenges of BWCs suggests that those concerns may be unwarranted or that the issues can be addressed through a careful, deliberate planning and implementation process. For example, many professional organizations have taken steps to address privacy-related concerns. The International Association of Chiefs of Police (IACP) held a national forum on body-worn cameras and violence against women and issued a report with policy and practice recommendations for recording female assault victims.[31] Moreover, current research has failed to produce evidence that BWCs cause officers to become less proactive (e.g., depolicing),[32] though several studies have reported increased arrest activity among BWC officers (suggesting that the cameras may impinge officers' use of discretion).[33] Initial officer buy-in can sometimes be problematic, and some agencies have overcome resistance to BWCs by offering a financial incentive to officers who volunteer to wear a camera.[34] White et al. found that many of the difficulties associated with BWC deployment, from officer resistance to prosecutors' failure to use the footage in criminal prosecutions, can be avoided by following the planning and implementation guidelines published by the US Department of Justice (see discussion later in chapter 5).[35] They concluded, "Body-worn camera program implementation comes with a high degree of difficulty. Poor BWC deployment will not only fail to achieve the stated program goals, but the technology may actually *create* additional harms for officers, citizens, and other stakeholders. As a result, BJA developed BWC implementation resources grounded in principles that are widely recognized as important for successful program implementation. The current study suggests that close adherence to those principles may produce high levels of integration and acceptance of BWCs among a diverse group of important stakeholders."[36]

Characteristics of the Innovators

Wejnert notes that characteristics of the innovation (BWCs) alone are not sufficient to explain diffusion patterns. Features of the innovators themselves, in this case police departments (and officers), also influence the rate of diffusion.[37]

SOCIETAL ENTITY OF INNOVATORS AND THEIR SOCIAL NETWORKS

The societal entity of innovators refers to the size of adopters: individual actors, small collective groups (e.g., group of friends), or a large collective group. In this case, the societal entity of innovators is quite large and is made up of nearly eighteen thousand local and state law enforcement agencies in the United States that employ approximately eight hundred thousand sworn officers.[38] Innovators maintain relationships with one another through a variety of social networks that can include face-to-face interactions as well as both formal and informal organizational networks. These connections represent the primary means by which innovators communicate information regarding an innovation. The large collective of US police departments communicate through a variety of networks, including informal relationships with nearby agencies and partners (e.g., word-of-mouth), through attendance at local trainings and conferences, through regional associations, and through national-level meetings such as the annual conferences of the International Association of Chiefs of Police,[39] Major Cities Chiefs

Association,[40] and the Center for Problem-Oriented Policing.[41] Several aspects of these networks warrant further discussion.

The President's Commission on Law Enforcement and the Administration of Justice recommended that all states establish a Peace Officer Standards and Training Commission (or POST) to develop statewide standards for police officer training and certification and to offer that training on a recurring basis.[42] Nearly all states now have a POST board. Importantly, the POST can serve as a central information source on a wide range of law enforcement topics, including new technologies such as BWCs. As an illustration, the California POST issues a monthly update that reviews timely issues related to police practice, and it includes a California state legislative update.[43] The May 2018 monthly report includes an update on Assembly Bill 459, which would "exempt video and audio files from a body-worn camera created by a peace officer of a state or local law enforcement agency that depict any victim of rape, incest, domestic violence, or child abuse from disclosure pursuant to the act, unless the victim or victims depicted provide express written consent."[44] POST boards can serve as an effective communication network regarding BWCs.

Also, leadership organizations in law enforcement in the United States, including the IACP and the Police Executive Research Forum (PERF), often offer important information and guidance on new technology. Both IACP and PERF were among the first organizations to provide guidance on police BWCs. In September 2013, PERF held a one-day conference on BWCs, resulting in the publication of an important report that includes dozens of specific policy and practice recommendations.[45] The IACP annual meetings, with attendance routinely over ten thousand, frequently includes panels on BWCs, and in 2016, IACP released a model BWC policy.[46] Also, the Fraternal Order of Police, the largest police union in the United States, with more than 330,000 members,[47] has issued a document detailing recommended policy and practice with BWCs.[48] Last, the Bureau of Justice Assistance offers a wide range of training and technical assistance related to BWCs, including a National

Body-Worn Camera Toolkit and a national training and technical assistance team.[49] These are just a few of the innovator networks that serve to disseminate information on BWCs.

FAMILIARITY WITH THE INNOVATION

Wejnert states that the "familiarity associated with an innovation relates to how radical it is."[50] In simple terms, the more novel the innovation, the slower the rate of diffusion. As the novelty of an innovation decreases, its rate of diffusion is likely to increase. There are a variety of things that can increase familiarity with an innovation. Certainly, the social networks just described represent important mechanisms for disseminating information on BWCs. There are also a variety of other law enforcement advocacy groups and websites that share information on new technologies, such as the Law Enforcement Executive Forum, PoliceOne, and the Police Policy Studies Council.[51] There are three additional information sources that have served to increase familiarity with BWCs. The first is the media. A quick Google search on "police body cameras" results in more than 123 million hits. When a police department deploys BWCs, it is frequently covered by the local news.[52] The publication of a research study has, in some cases, drawn national media attention.[53] Certainly, the recording of an officer-involved shooting on a BWC—or the failure to activate prior to a shooting—generates national headlines.[54] And there have been excellent reviews of the benefits and limitations of police BWCs in the media, such as an interactive video segment in the *New York Times*.[55]

Body-worn camera vendors are also a source of information on the innovation. Perhaps the best example is Axon (formerly TASER International), the most popular manufacturer of police BWCs.[56] Axon is very proactive in its marketing and advertising, and it has no doubt played a role in increasing the familiarity of its BWC, as well as its cloud-based storage system (Evidence.com). Company representatives attend local and national conferences, including the annual IACP conference. The company also supports local, state, and regional law enforcement leadership organizations. For example, Axon is a platinum-level sponsor of the Arizona Association of Chiefs of Police (AACOP).[57] In addition, Axon routinely issues press releases regarding equipment purchases and uses of its device in the field. Also, the Axon website is designed to provide detailed information on the technology (and to increase familiarity). The same can also be said about other BWC vendors, such as VIEVU (which was purchased by Axon in May 2018), WatchGuard, and Motorola.[58]

Last, researchers are an important mechanism for increasing familiarity with BWCs (see chapters 2 and 3). Certainly, the publication of the results from the Rialto (California) study increased familiarity with BWCs.[59] Research on officer perceptions of BWCs (innovator attitudes) have been especially relevant to this component of the diffusion of innovation framework. Wesley Jennings and colleagues found that over 60 percent of Orlando police officers believed their agency should deploy BWCs to all officers.[60] Officers across the Phoenix and Tempe (Arizona) and Spokane (Washington) Police Departments also reported positive perceptions of BWCs before and after deployment.[61] In fact, the improved perceptions of BWCs after deployment suggest that innovator acceptance of a technology increases as familiarity increases.

STATUS: PERSONAL AND SOCIOECONOMIC CHARACTERISTICS
OF THE INNOVATOR

Wejnert notes that there are aspects of individual innovators that can also influence diffusion patterns, especially if an early adopter has prominence in the network.[62] In the social network of police departments, there is a general correlation between department size and department status (e.g., the New York and Los Angeles Police Departments). However, this is not always the case. Some police departments have long traditions of being "on the cutting edge," regardless of their size (i.e., *personal characteristics* that favor innovation). Moreover, there may be regional cultural differences that come into play. For example, the West and Southwest tend to be more progressive with regard to city and political governance, compared to the more traditional northeastern and southern regions of the country. Wejnert also highlights the role of *socioeconomic characteristics* of the adopter. That is, the diffusion of an innovation is often strongly influenced by the "objective feasibilities" of the innovation itself, such as the financial costs of the innovation.[63]

In the case of BWCs, many of these issues have come into play and influenced the diffusion of the technology. BWCs gained significant attention in August 2013, when Judge Shira Scheindlin, of the federal district court in Manhattan, ordered the NYPD to deploy cameras as part of her ruling in the stop, question, and frisk case.[64] The Mesa and Phoenix Police Departments were early adopters of BWCs (in 2013), and both partnered with researchers to conduct evaluations of the camera programs.[65] The LAPD began its BWC program in August 2015,[66] and by mid-2018, it had more than eight thousand cameras deployed. Moreover, the early diffusion of the technology was certainly tied to the "objective feasibilities" of the innovation (i.e., cost), as available data indicate that BWCs are more popular among medium and large departments (compared to small).

Characteristics of the Environment

Wejnert states, "A fundamental element in adoption theory is recognition that innovations are not independent of their environmental context but that they rather evolve in a specific ecological and cultural context and their successful transfer depends on their suitability to the new environments they enter during diffusion."[67] In other words, environment matters.

GEOGRAPHIC SETTINGS AND POLITICAL CONDITIONS

Geography and political considerations often play an influential role in diffusion, and that has certainly been the case with police BWCs. Though adoption of BWCs had been increasing gradually through early 2014, interest in the technology exploded after the summer of 2014. Police killings of mostly minority citizens continued to draw national-level attention over the next few years (e.g., Tamir Rice, Walter Scott, Freddie Gray, Samuel Dubose, Justine Damond), and interest in police BWCs was shaped by this crisis in police-community relations. Police BWCs were a central tenet of President Obama's community policing plan,[68] and their value was highlighted in the final report recommendations of the President's Task Force on 21st Century Policing.[69] The diffusion of police BWCs is inextricably linked to the crisis in policing.

State and federal government action is another aspect of political conditions that has influenced diffusion. Since 2015, the US Department of Justice (DOJ) has awarded nearly $70 million in grant funding to 337 law enforcement agencies, resulting in the deployment of approximately seventy thousand BWCs. Numerous states have taken legislative action to influence the deployment of BWCs. In 2015, the state legislature in North Carolina mandated the use of police BWCs, and in 2017, Nevada passed a similar measure.[70] The Urban Institute has created an online resource, called the "Police Body-Worn Camera Legislations Tracker," to provide a state-by-state review of existing laws governing a range of BWC-related issues, including activation requirements, rules governing public access and release of footage, and mandated data-storage time.[71] The geopolitical landscape in the United States has played a significant role in BWC diffusion.

SOCIETAL CULTURE

Societal culture often can play an influential role in diffusion of an innovation. Laws, values, and norms can either facilitate or hinder the adoption patterns of an innovation. There are two aspects of culture that are especially relevant for examination of technology in policing. The first is the court system. The courts play a critical role through examination of cases that establish the parameters of BWC policy and practice. For example, the Boston police union filed an injunction in federal court to stop the leadership's planned rollout of BWCs.[72] The courts have also ruled on a range of controversial issues, such as the public release of footage,[73] the implications of failure to record an encounter or the deletion of video prior to a court case,[74] and whether BWC deployments must be negotiated as part of collective bargaining between the department and the officers' union.[75] The courts are also "consumers" of BWC footage, as the evidentiary value of cameras has implications for the processing and adjudication of criminal cases. The successful integration of BWC footage into court-case processing (by prosecutors and defense) will certainly influence the technology's rate of diffusion.

The second aspect of culture relevant for BWCs involves citizens' beliefs about the technology. What do citizens think about police BWCs? A number of studies have shown that citizens' support for BWCs is high, both among the general population and among citizens who have BWC-recorded encounters with police.[76] For example, White and colleagues conducted interviews with 279 citizens who had recent encounters with Tempe (Arizona) police officers and found high levels of acceptance: more than 90 percent of citizens agreed or strongly agreed that BWCs should be worn by all Tempe officers; nearly 80 percent agreed or strongly agreed that BWCs would make officers behave more professionally and citizens act more respectfully; and 84 percent agreed or strongly agreed that the benefits of BWCs outweigh the costs.[77] Similarly positive results have been reported among citizens who were recorded by police in Spokane (Washington),[78] Anaheim (California),[79] and Arlington (Texas).[80] Citizens' support for BWCs is likely to fuel the continued diffusion of the technology in policing. The diffusion of innovations framework helps us answer three of the questions posed at the beginning of this chapter, but to understand whether BWCs have been successful and how this real or perceived success will impact the future of the technology in policing, we turn to evidence-based policing.

Understanding BWCs through the Evidence-Based Policing Framework

Policing is an interesting animal. It has long been considered a craft, for which experience outweighs all else. However, the past few decades have ushered in a new framework for the field: evidence-based policing (EBP). Under an EBP approach, "police officers and staff create, review and use the best available evidence to inform and challenge policies, practices and decisions."[81] Using evidence has several advantages. In the book *Reducing Crime*, Jerry Ratcliffe states that "science and research can distinguish between good intentions and good programs."[82] Solid evidence not only helps agencies persuade politicians and the public to fund programs that work but also helps us avoid spending money on activities that have been shown not to work (Drug Abuse Resistance Education [DARE] and Scared Straight spring to mind). This section assesses BWCs using an EBP framework in an effort to determine whether the technology has been successful and whether BWCs will continue to impact policing long into the future.

Policing generally considers four types of research evidence in assessing success: scientific, organizational, professional, and stakeholder.[83] Table 4.2 describes each in the context of BWCs. We reviewed the first type—scientific evidence—in chapters 2 and 3. In assessing scientific evidence, it is important to understand that not all is created equal. There is a hierarchy of evidence when applied to policy decision-making, with systematic reviews and randomized controlled trials being considered among the strongest. Taking all of this into account, the scientific evidence shows that BWCs improve procedural justice, reduce citizen complaints, reduce officer use of force, and improve the detection and prosecution of crimes. This type of evidence also reveals costs, such as citizen privacy concerns and equipment and resource requirements. The scientific evidence is mixed when it comes to officer activity and does not yet provide an answer to police and policy makers who want to know whether BWCs have a depolicing effect. In cases like this, where the scientific evidence is not providing answers or simply not present, other types of evidence become instructive.

Organizational evidence—department data—is useful for assessing implementation success in individual agencies. This type of evidence

TABLE 4.2. Types of Evidence Relevant to BWCs

Scientific evidence	Scientific research on BWCs, such as the research reviewed in chapters 2 and 3, is normally found in peer-reviewed journal articles, books, and government and agency reports.
Organizational evidence	Police department data on BWCs and outcomes such as crime and arrest data, investigative interviews, victim surveys, financial breakdowns, complaint and use-of-force data, etc. are rarely analyzed yet can provide significant insight into the success of a BWC program for a particular agency.
Professional evidence	This is the less tangible, but nonetheless important, experiential evidence base of officers and analysts at all levels. Officers' experience with BWCs helps contextualize the success of an implementation effort.
Stakeholder evidence	Stakeholders (any group affected by a BWC program) also provide context and experiential evidence. As reviewed in chapter 3, listening to the concerns of stakeholder groups can help to avoid implementation problems and influence success.

is essential for two reasons. First, departments probably define *success* differently. For instance, one agency might have implemented BWCs for the purposes of increasing procedurally just policing and reducing officer use of force, while another may define a successful BWC program through improved crime detection and case outcomes. Articulating and measuring agency-level success apart from the general scientific evidence is important. Second, as we mention throughout the book, not all police departments are the same. BWC programs have different levels of *implementation effectiveness*. There is so much variation in BWC implementation that it is difficult to predict individual success on any metric. For example, it does not matter how much money you sink into technology if you have a rank and file who does not trust management and does not activate their cameras out of suspicion that their supervisors are "out to get them." Fortunately, departmental context can be assessed through the professional evidence.

Professional evidence, such as experience and intuition, is useful, especially when scientific evidence is lacking or not providing useful answers. The IACP and PERF organizations are useful sources for professional evidence. As previously mentioned in this chapter, both agencies were among the first to provide guidance on police BWCs through shared stories from the field.[84] Professional evidence can also be used to assess why BWCs were unsuccessful in specific departments and successful in others. For example, management can share stories about technological issues that otherwise would never make it into concrete data. However, it is important to understand that experience is vulnerable to bias and should be interpreted and applied with caution. Hence, professional evidence only ranks as a level 1 on the Maryland Scale of Scientific Methods (SMS).[85]

The last form of evidence relevant to BWCs comes from stakeholders. The groups affected by a BWC program are important players and will influence and help determine whether a BWC program is successful. The limited evidence available on stakeholders' perceptions of BWCs shows that, overall, they feel the programs are successful but with notable costs. As reviewed in chapter 3, Todak and colleagues recommend early and consistent engagement with police unions, neighboring police departments, prosecutors and public defenders, courts, city leaders, fire and rescue, and citizen and advocacy groups. They report that stakeholder evidence is essential to the success of BWC programs.

One particularly useful tool for assessing BWC evidence is the EMMIE (effect, mechanism, moderators, implementation, economic cost) framework. The EMMIE framework was developed by British researchers to examine not only effectiveness of policing interventions but also mechanisms, moderators, implementation factors, and cost implications.[86] In table 4.3, we apply EMMIE to BWCs. It should be clear after reading this book and assessing the four types of evidence discussed in this section that BWCs have been successful in improving a number of key outcomes. Mechanisms to consider include officer compliance and policy differences. Unfortunately, when it comes to moderators that influence whether BWCs will and will not work, we do not yet have adequate evidence from any source to answer with confidence. A successful implementation depends on a thorough review of stakeholder needs and priorities, addressing citizen and officer privacy

TABLE 4.3. The EMMIE Framework

Factor	Question posed	BWC application
Effect	What is the impact on key outcomes?	• improved procedural justice • reduced citizen complaints • reduced officer use of force • improved detection and prosecution of crimes • inconclusive on officer activity
Mechanism	How is the intervention supposed to work?	• officer compliance important • department policy differences important
Moderators	Where will it work and not work?	• more evidence needed
Implementation	What do you need to consider to make it work?	• stakeholder priorities and needs • citizen privacy concerns • officer privacy concerns • internal policy considerations
Economic cost	How much will it cost?	• substantial costs associated with equipment, storage, and resources • limited scientific evidence suggests costs could be offset by savings in citizen complaint cases and improved case outcomes

concerns, and developing a policy that both takes into account best practices and is sensitive to the local context. And finally, cost can be substantial, but there is limited evidence that costs are offset by savings in investigating and litigating citizen complaints and through improved case outcomes.

We have applied the evidence-based policing framework in an effort to address a fourth question about BWCs: have they achieved their desired effect? Viewed through the EBP perspective, we see that this is actually a complex question that belies a simple yes or no answer. In fact, the answer to this question depends on whom you ask, which effect you are focused on, and which evidence you consider. EBP encourages, as we have done throughout this book, weighing all the evidence—scientific, organizational, professional, and stakeholder—to assess the success of BWCs on both a technology-wide and department-specific scale. In doing so, consider the authenticity, credibility, representativeness, and context of all the available sources of evidence.

Conclusion

Both the diffusion of innovation and evidence-based policing frame-works provide a lens for examining and understanding the spread of BWCs in policing. With the diffusion of innovation framework, the characteristics of the innovation (public and private consequences, costs and benefits of BWCs), the innovators (societal entity/networks, familiarity, status), and the environment (geographic and political considerations, society) all explain the rapid diffusion of BWCs over the past few years. The technology has deep implications for police and numerous other stakeholders. The costs are significant, but so are the benefits. And the benefits tap into critical elements of the role and responsibilities of police. Key aspects of the police themselves explain the rapid diffusion, from their informal and formal social networks to mechanisms for increasing familiarity. Last, the environment has facilitated rapid diffusion, from the political context surrounding BWCs to widespread community support.

Through an evidence-based policing framework, we see that BWCs, for the most part, have achieved their desired effect. All four types of evidence tend to tell a roughly similar story: BWCs work but not without substantial privacy and economic costs. Moreover, the degree of effectiveness varies considerably based on the outcome and the agency under study. From both of these lenses, the rapid dispersion of BWCs in policing is both logical and understandable. Barring any unforeseen dramatic changes in these factors, both frameworks predict continued diffusion of BWCs in policing.

5

Charting a Course for Body-Worn Cameras in the Twenty-First Century

Much of *Cops, Cameras, and Crisis* has been focused on the past and present. How did we get to where we are today with this technology (chapter 1)? What does the existing body of research tell us about the benefits and drawbacks of police BWCs (chapters 2 and 3)? Can the rapid diffusion of BWCs be explained by existing frameworks (chapter 4)? Notably, the application of the diffusion of innovation and evidence-based policing frameworks in chapter 4 also allows us to begin to think about the future. In this last chapter, we continue to look forward. We first turn to a discussion of the next set of challenges police departments will have to address with BWCs. These second-level issues demonstrate that, even after BWC deployment, the degree of difficulty with this technology remains high. While the challenges described in chapter 3 are well-known, these latest obstacles are not as well understood, and the evidence base on how to successfully overcome them is thin at best. Nevertheless, these emerging challenges threaten a police department's ability to achieve the benefits described in chapter 2. In particular, we highlight three emerging challenges: activation compliance among officers; managing public expectations about the potential of BWCs; and technological advances that push BWCs into new areas (e.g., facial recognition, "big data," real-time streaming). Certainly other emerging challenges exist, and we do not mean to minimize them. But from our perspective, the aforementioned three obstacles represent the most serious emerging threats to a successful BWC program.

Next, we return to the importance of proper planning and implementation. We have made the case throughout this book that BWCs have tremendous potential to generate important benefits for police and their communities. However, those benefits are by no means guaranteed, and there are considerable hurdles that must be overcome if those benefits are to be realized. Failure to implement a BWC program properly not only will short-circuit the potential to achieve positive outcomes but may also generate harm for officers, the department, the community, and the relationship between the two. That harm could play out in the form of a negative impact on officer morale (e.g., views of organizational justice) and proactivity,[1] citizen misunderstanding and backlash toward the technology,[2] and failure to use BWC footage by prosecutors and the courts.[3] The US Department of Justice (DOJ) has developed resources to facilitate proper BWC planning and implementation, and we devote significant attention to those resources. We make the case that adherence to the DOJ guidelines will help organizations avoid the major pitfalls associated with BWCs (including those that are just emerging) and will increase the likelihood of experiencing successful outcomes. In the final part of the chapter, we offer some parting thoughts on the future of BWCs in policing. Now to the emerging challenges.

Three Emerging Challenges for BWC Adopters

Challenge 1: Monitoring Activation Compliance

Over the past few years, there have been numerous cases where officers have not activated their body-worn camera during a citizen encounter. In simple terms, there should have been a BWC recording of the encounter, but there was not. The most controversial cases involve a police shooting, like the death of Justine Damond.[4] There are three potential explanations for an officer's failure to activate. First, the officer may simply have forgotten. There is clearly a muscle memory aspect to BWCs, and it may take time for officers, especially veteran officers, to routinize the use of BWCs. An officer who has been on the street for fifteen years without a BWC will need some time to incorporate the device into his or her daily workday habits. Second, the decision not to activate may be intentional. Perhaps the encounter is consensual or informal, and under policy, activation is not required. Or the citizen may ask the officer to deactivate the BWC (e.g., the citizen may want to provide information to the officer but will not do so while the BWC is activated). Alternatively, the officer may choose to keep the BWC off for more nefarious reasons (e.g., to engage in misconduct). Third, the officer simply may not have time to activate the BWC. Police-citizen encounters are very dynamic. The officer may observe criminal behavior and be forced to intervene immediately. Or what starts as an informal conversation with a citizen may quickly change into something more serious. In these circumstances, officers simply do not have time to activate without jeopardizing their safety (or the safety of others).

The failure to activate a BWC, regardless of the reason, can be problematic for a police department. Low activation compliance can undermine all the benefits generated by BWCs. Consider the impact on efforts to demonstrate transparency to the community. Clearly, there is no added evidentiary value if there is no video. Can we expect citizen and officer behavior to improve if the camera is not activated? Moreover, months or years of building community trust can be wiped out by one failure to activate in a critical incident. More generally, we view low activation compliance as a form of implementation failure. In plain terms, a program will not be effective if it is not implemented properly or fully, and BWCs are no exception.

Additionally, recent studies have linked high levels of activation compliance with important outcomes such as reductions in use of force and citizen complaints. For example, Barak Ariel et al. tied patterns in use of force to officer decisions on BWC activation: when officers activated the BWC at the start of citizen encounters and advised citizens of the BWC, use of force declined by 37 percent. When officers did not follow policy on activation and citizen notification, use of force actually increased by 71 percent.[5] Eric Hedberg and colleagues projected the impact of BWCs on citizen complaints had there been a higher activation rate among Phoenix officers and concluded, "if BWCs are employed as prescribed [i.e., 100 percent activation compliance], a majority of complaints against officers would be eliminated."[6] Additionally, the absence of a video when one should exist creates a perception problem for the department. In some cases, citizens may presume that the failure to activate was an intentional effort to hide misconduct. The absence of a video may also impact prosecutor decisions to file charges, as well as subsequent court rulings on evidence. Some experts have raised concern about a new "CSI effect" among citizens (especially those serving on a jury), whereby there is an expectation that a movie-quality video will exist for every encounter, and when there is no such video, then "it didn't happen" (see the later section in this chapter).

There have been a handful of studies of BWC activation compliance, and the results are mixed. In perhaps the first (and best) study, Charles Katz et al. examined compliance among Phoenix police officers over a fourteen-month period in 2013–14.[7] The compliance rate varied significantly over time, peaking at 42 percent in the second month of the study period and declining notably over time. Altogether, activation compliance was about 30 percent—meaning that in 70 percent of the incidents where there should have been an activation, there was none. Compliance rates also varied significantly by call type, ranging from a high of 47.5 percent in domestic violence offenses to a low of 6.5 percent in traffic offenses.[8] The Denver Office of the Independent Monitor, which provides oversight of the Denver Police Department, reported that fewer than half of use-of-force incidents involving officers with BWCs were actually recorded.[9] The Mesa (Arizona) Police Department conducted a one-year study of BWCs under two separate activation policies. During the first six months, the policy was restrictive and required officers to record all formal encounters with citizens. During the second six months, the department adopted a more discretionary activation policy. The department reported that activations declined by 42 percent under the more discretionary policy.[10] Both McClure et al. and White et al. examined individual officer activation rates and found a wide range, from as low as 0 percent to over 75 percent (see figures 5.1

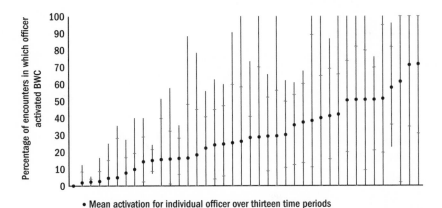

FIGURE 5.1. Individual officer activation rates (McClure et al., *Perceptions of Police*)

and 5.2).[11] The similarity in individual officer compliance rates among the two different departments is notable and suggests a consistent pattern of low, medium, and high activators among officers. Daniel Lawrence and colleagues extended the McClure et al. analysis, noting that average activation rates increased notably over time (from 3 percent to 54 percent) and that activation rates were highest for calls involving serious crimes.[12]

Given the consequences of failure to activate both generally and in critical incidents, it is vitally important for police departments to routinely monitor compliance. The easiest path to institutionalizing activation compliance is to build it into BWC policy as a mandatory auditing function of first-line supervisors. Our view is that activation is an exercise in discretion, and five decades of research highlight the importance of administrative policy for effective guidance/control of officers' use of discretion.[13] In plain terms, officers adhere to policies that are detailed, clear, understood, and enforced. Research has demonstrated this finding across a wide range of police decisions, from use of force and automobile pursuits to arrest decisions.[14] A good BWC policy is enforced. And good BWC policy will lead to good BWC practice.

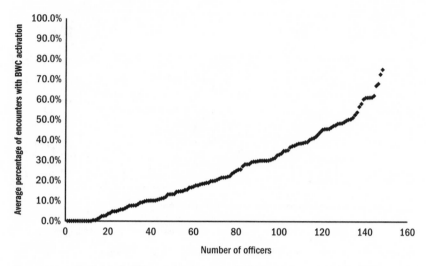

FIGURE 5.2. Individual officer activation rates (White, Gaub, and Todak, "To Record or Not to Record?")

In Box 5.1, Chief Paul Noel of the New Orleans Police Department discusses the importance of an auditing program, both for maintaining community trust and for ensuring the success of the BWC program. Many police departments have built this auditing function into their BWC policy as a responsibility of first-line supervisors. For example, Michael White and colleagues examined the BWC policies of more than two hundred agencies that have received federal funding for BWCs.[15] They note that the vast majority of federally funded agencies require supervisors to conduct periodic or random reviews of their subordinates' BWC footage. In many cases, the supervisor review is strictly to assess compliance with BWC policy. Are officers activating the BWC when they should? Are they properly tagging videos? If required, are they notifying citizens of the BWC? In other cases, some departments also allow supervisors to assess officer performance more generally as part of this auditing function. In fact, White and colleagues reported that 85 percent of federally funded agencies give supervisors the authority to view BWC footage for general performance review.

BOX 5.1

"Body-worn cameras do more than simply capture videos of a police encounters. They help us establish and maintain public trust, but with that trust comes great responsibility for law enforcement leaders. Community members expect that if an agency uses cameras, they will be used in every encounter. Police leaders need to establish an auditing system to make sure their officers are activating their body-worn cameras in every encounter, not just most of the time. A robust auditing system and clear policy and procedures are critical to the success of any agency's body-worn camera program."
—Paul M. Noel, Chief of Operations, New Orleans Police Department (authors' interview)

We do acknowledge a tension between the need to monitor activation compliance on a routine basis and the resources required for such a monitoring program. This task can become especially onerous for first-line supervisors. For example, let us assume Sergeant A has ten officers under his command, and each officer generates three hours of video per shift, or a total of 30 hours of video per day. If officers work a four-day week ("four tens"), that is 120 hours of video generated per week. How much time should a sergeant devote to reviewing video? Sergeants perform a variety of tasks that are vital to the successful day-to-day functioning of the organization, from reviewing reports and mentoring young officers to providing the first level of accountability. The added responsibility of reviewing BWC footage will necessarily take up time that could be devoted to these other tasks. Geoffrey Alpert and Kyle McLean also highlight the importance of monitoring compliance but warn of the difficulties in doing so as a result of the role of officer discretion (officers choosing not to activate for legitimate reasons), technological limitations (data systems not integrated), and other types of human error (officers simply forgetting or not having time to activate).[16] Notably, many of the BWC vendors have developed automated activation features to take the human element out of the activation equation (e.g., if the officer pulls the gun or TASER from the holster, the BWC is automatically activated).[17] The automated activation feature is intriguing, but at the time of this writing, vendors are, for the most part, still pilot-testing these technologies.

Agency leaders should address a few important questions as they design their auditing program. First, how should those videos be selected? Certain categories of video should have automatic review, such as those involving a use of force, injury, citizen complaint, pursuit, or other serious police action. Beyond the cases subject to automatic review, we recommend a random selection process. The principles of randomization allow the department to make assumptions regarding the representativeness of the videos. Also, the random process conveys to officers that every video has an equal chance of being selected for review. The random selection of videos could also be stratified by squad, shift, or geographic area to ensure that videos from all relevant units, shifts, or areas are selected. For example, a lieutenant who oversees five squads could randomly select fifteen videos per week; or the same lieutenant could randomly select three videos from each squad per week (ensuring that videos from each squad are selected). The selection could also be purposive, as videos from certain officers (probationers or those flagged by an early intervention system) or shifts (high activity) could be selected each week.

Second, what actions should be taken if a sergeant documents an officer's failure to activate during an encounter or if a sergeant identifies an officer who routinely fails to activate? Many departments have implemented a graduated scale of discipline approach whereby officers receive a warning, coaching, or additional training before more formal discipline is considered. Last, procedures should be in place in the event a supervisor observes conduct that is inappropriate or violates policy. These are important questions that the department leadership must resolve in order to effectively monitor officers' use of BWCs.

Challenge 2: Managing Public Expectations

The management of public expectations regarding BWCs is a significant challenge for police departments. One aspect of this challenge is the potential for BWCs to produce a new version of the "CSI effect." "CSI effect" is a term coined by criminal justice practitioners to describe jurors' reactions to forensic evidence such as DNA, derived primarily from the depiction of forensic evidence in the television series *CSI* (where forensic evidence is collected in every case, test results are returned immediately, the suspect is identified from the forensic evidence, and the case is closed within sixty minutes).[18] As a result of the exposure to this popular television show and its spin-offs, criminal defense attorneys have noted that jurors tend to be universally accepting and uncritical of forensic evidence as infallible. Prosecutors, on the other hand, have complained that jurors will not render a guilty verdict unless forensic evidence is presented at trial, even if it is not relevant for the case.[19] The same challenge could arise for BWCs: the cameras will become so normalized that jurors will be reluctant to convict someone unless there is BWC footage. Officers have expressed similar concerns in a handful of attitudinal studies, suggesting that citizens or jurors will view the absence of footage as evidence of an attempt to cover up police misbehavior.[20]

Similarly, there is concern that the general public may not fully understand the limitations of body-worn cameras. BWCs do not provide movie-quality picture and audio, particularly when the officer is in close quarters, is involved in a physical struggle, or is in a foot pursuit.[21] Also, the device is attached to an officer's uniform, sunglasses, or hat by a magnet or clip, and it may fall off during a chase or struggle.[22] The placement of the device (either on the officer's chest, temple, or lapel) can result in a distorted or obstructed view of what actually happened, leading to perspective bias.[23] Additionally, officers have expressed concern regarding the ability of media, courtroom actors (e.g., defense attorneys and jurors), and the public to conduct slow-motion review of footage (or simply to review it multiple times), which could lead to "Monday-morning quarterbacking" of officers' split-second decisions.[24]

Finally, the public's expectations of release of footage may be unreasonable. All police departments have a mechanism for public request and release of BWC footage, but there is wide variation in the laws that govern release. In Washington State, where public records laws are liberal, the Seattle Police Department responded to a wave of public records requests by redacting nearly all footage and uploading it to a public YouTube channel.[25] Police departments often have the authority to withhold footage in certain situations, such as during active investigations, and available data indicate that many states have passed legislation to restrict public access to BWC footage in some way.[26] In 2016, for example, the North Carolina General Assembly passed House Bill 972, which classified BWC and dashboard-camera footage as part of officers' personnel records, and a court order is now required before BWC footage can be released.[27] The Las Vegas Metropolitan Police Department has developed a detailed policy on the release of BWC footage to the public, which includes specific limits on access and fees for the preparation of released footage.[28] Moreover, departments may vary considerably with regard to how and when they release the video, especially when use of force in involved. The LAPD recently implemented a forty-five-day release policy for critical incidents, such as officer-involved shootings.[29] The Seattle Police Department policy manual states that within seventy-two hours of an officer-involved shooting, the department will release a "representative and relevant sample" of available video.[30] The Las Vegas Metropolitan Police Department also has a seventy-two-hour release policy for officer-involved shootings. The Seattle and Las Vegas Metropolitan Police Departments release raw video at a press conference, with police officials present to narrate the events and answer questions. The LAPD, on the other hand, releases a Hollywood-like video production that includes raw BWC footage, narration, and commentary from department officials.[31]

Ultimately, it is the responsibility of the local police department to proactively engage with local stakeholders and the community to manage expectations about BWCs. This discussion should start early in the BWC planning process and continue throughout implementation. The dialogue should be ongoing after deployment as well. Communication is key! Finally, each department should devise a BWC release policy that is consistent with state law, fits its local needs, keeps citizens informed, and dispels the sometimes unreasonable expectations of the public regarding BWCs.

Challenge 3: Technological Advances Driving BWCs into New Areas

The first two emerging challenges just described deal with human-related issues: officers' use of BWCs (or, to be more precise, officers' failure to use BWCs) and citizens' misconceptions about various aspects of the technology. The last emerging challenge we would like to discuss is tied to the technology itself, particularly how BWCs will be pushed into new, uncharted territory via the data that are captured by the cameras. Police BWCs record vast amounts of data, often measured in petabytes,[32] and that data must be stored securely either locally (on department or city-owned servers) or on the cloud (via third-party vendors) for set periods of time determined by state law. Margaret Hu notes that technological advances will complicate the data-collection aspect of BWCs, as the "next generation of smart police body cameras increasingly attempt to integrate live-streaming video with facial recognition and other artificial intelligence tools, such as automated analytics and database screening capacities."[33] There are a few aspects of the emerging data-collection challenge worthy of discussion. The first is data security and the extent to which BWC storage systems are vulnerable to cyberattack. Peter Swire and Jesse Woo note, "BWCs already generate, and will increasingly generate, a great amount of video footage and related content. In our era of increasingly effective facial recognition, this video footage generates a vast amount of personally identifiable information, with consequent privacy issues. Over time, the volume of video footage will increase enormously, creating challenging cybersecurity issues for the data that is stored, often in the cloud. Cities and police departments will face substantial challenges in managing these privacy and cybersecurity issues."[34] The potential for cyberattacks on police BWC data-storage systems represents a significant concern, as hacked footage could be altered, deleted, stolen, or released to the public—all of which would violate the chain-of-custody protections for criminal investigation/prosecution and could threaten thousands of criminal cases. The citizen privacy concerns are equally troubling, as images of victims and children, as well as other protected, personally identifiable information, could become publicly available.

The cybersecurity vulnerabilities of BWCs were highlighted at a 2018 conference where one security consultant reported on his research testing five different BWC models. He found significant security problems in four of the five models and concluded, "The vulnerabilities would allow an attacker to download footage off a camera, edit things out or potentially make more intricate modifications, and then re-upload it, leaving no indication of the change. Or an attacker could simply delete footage they don't want law enforcement to have."[35]

Jay Stanley, a senior policy analyst with the ACLU, notes, "The fact that some law enforcement evidence-collecting devices can be hacked evokes some true nightmare scenarios. If there aren't reliable ways of ensuring that such equipment meets strong security standards, then something is deeply broken."[36] Swire and Woo suggest, however, that best-practice standards developed for the "Internet of Things" (IoT) by Microsoft, the Broadband Internet Technical Advisory Group (BITAG), and the Federal Trade Commission (FTC) can be extended to BWCs and can provide a roadmap for police departments to ensure BWC data security.[37] On the basis of our collective experience, most police departments have not fully considered the cybersecurity issues surrounding their BWC data-storage systems. That needs to change.

The second challenge involves how the data collected by BWCs can be used. Hu warns BWCs may become a vehicle for the collection and analysis of mass biometric metadata. Metadata is "data about data," such as "the time of a telephone call or the email addresses of a recipient and sender."[38] Biometric data involves computerized information unique to individuals, such as fingerprints, DNA, or facial images. Police departments across the United States (and abroad) are increasingly reliant on biometric data to guide their decision-making. Forensic analysis of fingerprints and DNA has long been a part of police criminal investigations, and facial recognition is increasingly used in both threat assessment (e.g., at the Super Bowl) and after-the-fact criminal investigations (e.g., when Baltimore police used facial recognition after the 2015 riots to identify suspects).[39] Police BWC programs collect and store biometric data, most notably facial images. Hu notes that the Edward Snowden disclosure in 2013 of a National Security Agency (NSA) mass surveillance program of telephone metadata led to the passage of the USA FREEDOM Act, which was designed to tighten the regulations around bulk phone metadata collection.[40] But Hu warns that the USA FREEDOM Act does not extend to biometric data, in a way that is "similar to the lack of legal restraint on bulk telephony metadata collection prior to the Snowden disclosures. There is currently a lack of legal restraint on the scope and potential applications of bulk biometric data collection initiatives."[41] Hu argues that BWC data could serve as the foundation for systematized biometric data analysis that would provide law enforcement and the intelligence community with mass, suspicionless surveillance of US citizens.[42]

The third aspect of the BWC data collection challenge has been touched on in the previous two aspects: the potential for law enforcement to connect BWCs to facial recognition software. Facial recognition systems use algorithms, typically based on facial geometry, (1) to detect and extract patterns from an image and (2) to match those patterns with templates stored in a database.[43] In effect, the facial image is translated into a mathematical representation that can be compared to other mathematical representations (faces) in a reference database. Systems can also generate a percentage likelihood of a match. Facial recognition systems can be broadly classified into two general uses: identification (who is this person?) and verification (is this person who he or she claims to be?). Both of these systems have obvious value for police departments, but to date, law enforcement applications of facial recognition software have been limited because of cost (return on investment), accuracy of the systems, and objections from civil rights groups. For example, John Woodward et al. have noted, "environmental factors such as differences in camera angle, direction of lighting, facial expression, and other parameters can have significant effects on the ability of the systems to recognize individuals."[44] In the early 2000s, the Tampa (Florida) Police Department deployed a facial recognition system in Ybor City (a popular tourist spot) using a gallery database of wanted suspects and runaway children. After two years, their system failed to produce a single match.[45] In the wake of the 9/11 terrorist attacks, Boston's Logan Airport tested two separate facial recognition systems with volunteers who had their facial images entered into a gallery database and who posed as "terrorists" entering airport security checkpoints. Of the 249 opportunities to detect the presence of a "terrorist," the systems identified just 153 individuals, for a hit rate of 61.4 percent.[46]

The potential linkage between facial recognition software and police BWCs has led to a contentious debate. On the one hand, several recent cases have demonstrated the expanded use and value of facial recognition in law enforcement. For example, police used facial recognition to determine the identity of the suspect in the *Capital Gazette* newsroom shooting.[47] In April 2018, Axon (the largest vendor of police BWCs) announced the creation of a corporate board to study the ethics and expansion of artificial intelligence, including facial recognition, with its products.[48] Upon announcement of the Axon corporate board, forty-two civil rights and privacy groups sent a joint letter to the company voicing their concerns. The letter stated,

Certain products are categorically unethical to deploy. Chief among these is real-time face recognition analysis of live video captured by body-worn cameras. Axon must not offer or enable this feature. Real-time face recognition would chill the constitutional freedoms of speech and association, especially at political protests. In addition, research indicates that face recognition technology will never be perfectly accurate and reliable, and that accuracy rates are likely to differ based on subjects' race and gender. Real-time face recognition therefore would inevitably misidentify some innocent civilians as suspects. These errors could have fatal consequences—consequences that fall disproportionately on certain populations. Real-time face recognition could also prime officers to perceive individuals as more dangerous than they really are and to use more force than the situation requires. No policy or safeguard can mitigate these risks sufficiently well for real-time face recognition ever to be marketable.[49]

In July 2018, the ACLU released results from a test using Amazon facial recognition software to compare members of Congress to a publicly available "mug shot" database of twenty-five thousand individuals who had been arrested by police. The ACLU reported that twenty-eight congress members were incorrectly identified by the facial recognition software, and those who were incorrectly identified were disproportionately minorities.[50] In August 2018, Axon CEO Rick Smith acknowledged the limitations of facial recognition in a meeting with investors, stating, "It doesn't work well enough yet. The accuracy thresholds are not where they need to be to be making operational decisions off the facial recognition. . . . This is one where we think you don't want to be premature and end up either where you have technical failures with disastrous outcomes or . . . there's some unintended use-case where it ends up being unacceptable publicly in terms of long-term use of the technology."[51] Nevertheless, many experts view the merging of police BWCs with facial recognition and other "big data" systems as a real possibility in the future.[52] The National League of Cities argues (and we agree) that police departments should initiate conversations internally and externally about the potential use of facial recognition technology, particularly with regard to privacy, cost, and liability.[53] Concerns from local stakeholders should inform, if not dictate, future decisions that a police department makes with regard to the integration of facial recognition software and BWCs.

Road Map for Success: The US Department of Justice Best-Practice Implementation Guide

The difficulties associated with successful BWC program planning and implementation can be significant, as discussed in chapter 3. The new, emerging challenges described previously in this chapter represent new threats to a successful BWC program. The US Department of Justice is acutely aware of the challenges to planning, implementing, and managing a BWC program, and early on, it began efforts to provide guidance to agencies deploying the technology. For example, in February 2015 (six months after the death of Michael Brown in Ferguson, Missouri), the Bureau of Justice Assistance (BJA) hosted an "expert panel" at the White House to discuss the issues associated with police BWCs and to gather information that would create the foundation for a National Body-Worn Camera Toolkit.[54] One of us (White) facilitated the expert panel and is a primary author of the Toolkit. The complexity of issues surrounding BWCs was immediately evident to everyone in the room at the White House, and as a result, BJA along with a handful of subject-matter experts immediately set about developing resources that could guide agencies as they plan and deploy their BWC programs.

The BJA resources generally fall into two categories. First, BJA manages the US Department of Justice BWC funding program, called the Policy and Implementation Program (PIP).[55] The PIP program is the realization of former president Obama's December 2014 pledge to provide $75 million in funding for the deployment of fifty thousand BWC nationally. In the first four years of the program, BJA provided more than $70 million in funding to 337 law enforcement agencies, resulting in the deployment of just over seventy thousand BWCs nationally.[56] As part of the PIP program, BJA also funds a Training and Technical Assistance (TTA) team that provides support to agencies receiving funding. The TTA team, composed of representatives from CNA, the Center for Violence Prevention and Community Safety at Arizona State University, and Justice and Security Strategies,[57] offers a wide range of TTA services to facilitate successful planning and implementation of BWCs programs, including administrative policy review, webinars and podcasts, national and regional meetings, peer-to-peer meetings, a speaker's bureau, and monthly contacts.[58] The overall goal of the TTA team is to help funded agencies navigate the complexities of BWC program planning and development. All of the TTA resources are publicly available on its website,[59] and the TTA team will provide assistance with BWCs to any agency that asks, whether a recipient of federal funding or not.

The second set of BJA resources are available through the National Body-Worn Camera Toolkit.[60] The Toolkit, rolled out by BJA in May 2015, provides law enforcement agencies with a wide range of resources about BWCs, including the latest research, guidance on policy and training, and information on engagement with prosecutors, advocacy groups, citizens, and so on. The Toolkit is also heavily focused on proper planning and implementation, most notably through its "Law Enforcement Implementation Checklist."[61] The Checklist, which is grounded in principles drawn from the larger evidence base on successful program implementation in the criminal justice system,[62] including policing,[63] courts,[64] and corrections,[65] is designed to serve as a best-practices guide for successful planning and implementation of a BWC program.[66] The Checklist provides over two dozen steps for an agency to follow when implementing a BWC program. The Checklist centers on six core principles: learn the fundamentals and develop a plan; form a working group; develop policy; define the technology solution (procurement); communicate with and educate stakeholders; and execute phased rollout/implementation. Adherence to the best-practices guide should optimize the likelihood of successful BWC implementation. Successful implementation will, in turn, increase the potential for positive program outcomes.

BJA LAW ENFORCEMENT IMPLEMENTATION CHECKLIST
1. Learn the fundamentals and develop a plan
2. Form a working group
3. Develop policy
4. Define the technology solution (procurement)
5. Communicate with and educate stakeholders
6. Execute phased rollout/implementation

We devote significant attention to the BJA Checklist here, given (1) the high degree of difficulty associated with successful BWC program planning and implementation and (2) the consequences of planning and implementing poorly.

Learn the Fundamentals and Develop a Plan

An effective BWC program starts with careful planning.[67] Perhaps the most important first step of program planning centers on answering the "why" question. Why does the department want to deploy BWCs? What goal or goals is the department trying to accomplish? Is the goal to enhance the collection of evidence to support arrest and prosecution? Is it to improve the agency's relationship with the community? Is it to increase officer accountability? The goal(s) should drive the planning and implementation process, and BWC programs may look and function very differently based on the aims the department is seeking to achieve. Alpert and McLean note that many departments have adopted BWCs without establishing a clear goal for the program: "The rise in BWCs across the country has been plagued in part by a clear push for the technology to be implemented, but a clear or defined goal for success has been remarkably absent. . . . It is unwise, however, for a law

enforcement executive to get swept up in the BWC push without carefully evaluating his or her goals and policies."[68]

Second, the department should do its homework to make sure it has
a complete understanding of the benefits and limitations of BWCs, as
well as the costs and resources required to manage the program. "Learn
the fundamentals" means being an educated consumer. Agency leaders
should access all available information, and the National Body-Worn
Camera Toolkit representing an excellent starting point. It may also be
helpful for a department to reach out to peer and neighboring departments that have already deployed BWCs. Departments that have already
deployed BWCs are likely to have a wealth of lessons learned that they
can impart to a department just getting started (e.g., to use those peer
networks that form an important part of the diffusion of innovation
framework). The BJA Checklist also recommends that agency leaders
engage all relevant stakeholders in the local jurisdiction, both internal
and external, in the planning process. Internally, this would include the
rank and file, the officers' union, training staff, investigations, and information and technology units. Externally, the department should communicate with city leadership, criminal justice partners (especially the
prosecutor), and community leaders. Academic researchers may also be
useful for planning, implementation, and evaluation. Third, the Checklist also recommends identifying a project manager who will oversee
the day-to-day aspects of planning and serve as the "champion" of the
program. Last, the Checklist advises agency leaders to develop a written
project plan and timeline with milestones. This document will serve as
a guide for the department to follow during the next stages of the planning and implementation process.

Form a Working Group

The BJA Checklist advises that a department should create a BWC working group composed of internal stakeholders who will assume primary
responsibility for the planning and implementation process.[69] The BWC

working group should meet regularly (weekly or biweekly) to keep the planning and implementation process on track (e.g., to make sure that milestones are achieved and that the project timeline is maintained) and to discuss emerging challenges and identify solutions. All relevant units within the organization should have representation in this group, including agency leadership, command and first-line supervisors, patrol officers, union representatives, records management, information technology (IT), and legal and training staff.[70] Specialized units, such as investigations, SWAT, and anticrime (e.g., gang and narcotics), should also be represented if the agency plans to deploy BWCs beyond patrol. Though BWCs are generally well received by police (see chapter 2), there may be initial resistance, questions, or concerns within the department. Comprehensive participation at all stages of the planning process can help overcome initial internal resistance to the technology and will allow the working group to troubleshoot problems as they arise. Moreover, participation in the planning and implementation process should enhance longer-term buy-in with the technology through enhanced feelings of organizational justice,[71] as officers from the various units are given a voice in the process. The BWC working group should also engage with external stakeholders, especially city leaders (city council, mayor), downstream criminal justice actors (prosecutors, defense, courts), advocacy groups (ACLU, NAACP), and citizens (community and religious leaders, tenant associations, advisory boards, etc.). The rollout of a BWC program should be a surprise to no one, and the more input the department receives through the working group, the better.

Develop Policy

A clear, comprehensive, and enforced administrative policy is the centerpiece of a successful BWC program.[72] Five decades of police research have consistently documented the importance of administrative policy for guiding police officers' decision-making and their use of discretion across a range of field behaviors, including use of deadly force,[73] less lethal force,[74] high-speed pursuits,[75] use of police dogs,[76] foot pursuits,[77] and responses to domestic violence incidents.[78] Administrative policy is advocated by a wide range of organizations as an effective way to manage police decision-making, from the International Association of Chiefs of Police (IACP) and the American Bar Association (ABA) to the American Civil Liberties Union (ACLU). The Commission on Accreditation for Law Enforcement Agencies (CALEA) has built its entire accreditation process on administrative policy (see Box 5.2). Good policy is detailed and clear, understood by the officers, and enforced. Officers understand what is expected of them and what is prohibited, and if they violate policy, they know they will have to answer for that policy violation. This body of police research serves as a foundation for understanding the importance of BWC policy. Use of BWCs by officers is a police decision, like any other police decision. A BWC policy serves as a guide to those decisions. It conveys information to officers on key issues such as activation, deactivation, citizen notification, officer authority to review footage, and supervisor authority to review footage (e.g., auditing for compliance).

BOX 5.2

"CALEA Accreditation requires an agency to develop a comprehensive, well thought out, uniform set of *written directives*. This is one of the most successful methods for reaching administrative and operational goals, while also providing direction to personnel."
—CALEA (Commission on Accreditation for Law Enforcement Agencies), "Law Enforcement Accreditation"

A good BWC policy starts with a deliberate, inclusive policy development process. The BWC working group should begin with a review of relevant local and state laws, as well existing policies from leadership organizations in policing and peer/neighboring agencies. The BJA Body-Worn Camera Toolkit includes dozens of administrative policies and provides links to model policies from the International Association of Chiefs of Police (IACP) and the United Kingdom Home Office. The BJA Checklist places special attention on six core policy areas: video capture (activation, consent); video viewing (supervisor, officer); video use (evidence); video release (public access); video storage (downloading, chain of custody); and process/data audits and controls (compliance monitoring). Both line officers and their union should play a role in the policy development process and should provide input on key issues such as activation, officer discretion to deactivate, and supervisory review of BWC footage. Moreover, the BWC policy should be a "living document" that is reviewed and updated regularly based on changes in the law, available best practices, and local needs.

Relatedly, policy is also the foundation of the BJA BWC Policy and Implementation Program (PIP). Agencies that receive federal money for BWCs must go through an intensive policy review process devised by the TTA team. The centerpiece of the review process is the Policy Review Scorecard, an Excel-based tool that rates the comprehensiveness of a BWC policy across eleven general areas and forty-one specific policy issues.[79] Policies are rated by assessing whether or not each specific issue is addressed (0 or 1). For agencies that receive federal funding, seventeen of the forty-one issues are mandatory and must be covered in policy. To pass the policy review process, an agency must score an 80 percent or better (thirty-three of forty-one), with seventeen of seventeen on the mandatory items.[80] An agency receiving a federal grant can access 10 percent of its funds immediately, but the agency cannot access the remaining 90 percent until it has passed the policy review process. The premise here is simple: a good BWC program starts with a comprehensive BWC policy, and as we have said before, good BWC policy leads to good BWC practice.

Define the Technology Solution (Procurement)

Police departments often are required to adhere to a formal procurement process when they purchase equipment, BWCs included. The

BWC working group should assume primary responsibility of the procurement process. The procurement process should begin with an evaluation of the hardware and software needs/limitations of the agency (e.g., infrastructure issues, desired camera resolution), financial and resource constraints, and review of data-storage options (e.g., local servers or third-party cloud storage).[81] Decisions on these issues are outlined in a Request for Proposals (RFP) that is released to BWC vendors. Vendors (there are more than sixty in the market as of summer 2019) then submit bids in response to the RFP. The BWC working group should develop a bid review and scoring process that can guide vendor selection. Components of the bid review may include on-site vendor presentations or interviews, reference checks with other agencies that use the vendor, and field-testing of the vendor's product by officers in the department. The officers who pilot-test BWCs should report to the working group on their perceptions of the specific product, as this line-level feedback should inform the working group's decision-making process. As a resource, the PIP TTA team has developed a generic RFP to guide agencies through the procurement process.[82]

Communicate with and Educate Stakeholders

Open communication is a centerpiece of the BJA-recommended process.[83] There should be an internally focused marketing campaign that disseminates all aspects of the BWC program to the entire department, from program goals to anticipated deployment schedules. Members of the working group can also spread information about the program through more informal communication chains. Once again, the key is no surprises. An external communication plan with stakeholders outside the department is also important. External marketing can reduce concerns/questions among citizens, advocacy groups, and other downstream criminal justice actors. Working-group members can attend community group meetings, meet individually with prosecutors and judges, provide testimony and answer questions at city council meetings, and so on. The local media can also be a valuable partner by disseminating information about the BWC program. In fact, several police departments across the country have held a "media day" to publicize their rollout of the BWC program, to demonstrate how the technology works, and to answer questions about the program.[84]

Execute Phased Rollout/Implementation

The BJA Checklist highlights several key developments during the implementation of BWCs, including the training of officers, continued communication with stakeholders, and regular program monitoring.[85] Training for officers should include basic operation of the technology, such as activation and deactivation, battery life, proper tagging of videos, and downloading. But the BWC policy should also be a central feature of the training. Role-play training can convey key aspects of the policy in near-real-world scenarios. The PIP TTA team has developed a guide to facilitate effective BWC training.[86]

The Checklist also advises a phased-in deployment of BWCs rather than a one-time, agency-wide rollout. The deployment of BWCs is highly complex, even for an agency that has adhered to these principles. The phased rollout is more measured and provides additional flexibility to make adjustments as needed to the BWC program. Moreover, if an organization has partnered with a researcher to evaluate the BWC program, the phased rollout can allow for a rigorous research design, such as a randomized controlled trial (RCT). The RCT is considered the gold standard in research, as it permits researchers to draw definitive conclusions about the impact of BWCs on key outcomes.[87]

Last, the Checklist recommends ongoing assessment of BWC operations and outcomes, as well as periodic reviews of policy and training. The evidence on BWCs is constantly changing given the rapid, widespread diffusion of the technology. Changes in local, state, or federal law may require modifications to a BWC program. New technological advances may push BWCs into new areas. High-profile events may raise questions about aspects of a BWC policy. For example, Sacramento (California) police officers' decision to mute their BWCs after shooting a suspect led to public protest and outrage and fueled a national-level debate over proper BWC procedure in the aftermath of an officer-involved shooting.[88] In short, BWC programs should not be static—agencies should modify their policies and programs as our knowledge about BWCs improves. Departments need to stay on top of emerging issues, and they must be nimble with regard to modifying their program to reflect the latest in BWC policy and practice.

An Empirical Test of the US Department of Justice Best-Practice Implementation Guide

Researchers (including one of us) recently published an article offering a test of the DOJ guide.[89] The Tempe (Arizona) Police Department (TPD) engaged in a nearly two-year planning process that reflected the basic principles just described.[90] Researchers tested the impact of TPD's close adherence to the DOJ BWC guide on multiple indicators of integration and acceptance, among a diverse group of stakeholders. They examined officer perceptions through six waves of officer surveys pre- and postdeployment. The interviewed nearly three hundred citizen who had recent encounters with Tempe police officers, and they conducted focus groups/interviews with seventeen stakeholders outside the department (prosecutors, judges, fire/rescue, etc.). The researchers also examined trends in officer activity levels (self-initiated calls) and misdemeanor court-processing outcomes (guilty outcomes and case processing times). Their findings demonstrated strong integration and acceptance of BWCs across all three groups: officers, citizens, and external stakeholders. On the basis of the weight of the collective evidence, the researchers concluded that close adherence to the implementation guide can produce high levels of integration and acceptance of BWCs among a diverse group of important stakeholders.

Given that strong integration and acceptance of BWCs is a necessary precondition for experiencing positive outcomes (e.g., reductions in citizen complaints or use of force, enhancements in officer and citizen satisfaction, and enhanced criminal case processing), "police departments considering a BWC program would be well-advised to pay close attention to the BJA implementation resources."[91] Alpert and McLean concur in their essay, concluding, "It is easy to understand the pressures that law enforcement executives are under to adopt BWC programs quickly, but a methodical, measured approach as outlined by the BJA (2015) checklist is more likely to result in a program that accomplishes its goals, satisfies external stakeholders, and obtains the support of line-level officers."[92]

Summary

BWCs have tremendous potential to benefit police and citizens in important ways, from reductions in use of force and citizen complaints to enhanced perceptions of procedural justice. But proper planning and implementation is key. If a department rushes to deploy BWCs without full consideration of the issues, all of the potential benefits of BWCs will fall by the wayside. Officers will not use the cameras properly. Citizens' behavior will not be positively affected by the cameras. Prosecutors will not integrate the video and audio footage into their cases. There is a long history of implementation failure in criminal justice programming across police, courts, and corrections.[93] And there is great risk of implementation failure with BWCs, given the complexity of issues involved and the tremendous, long-term resource commitment required by the organization. We believe the DOJ BWC implementation guide offers a road map to successful BWC planning and implementation. Police departments can accomplish two important goals by following the DOJ BWC implementation guide. First, they can reduce the risk of implementation failure. Second, they can optimize the likelihood of achieving positive outcomes.

Conclusion

Cops, Cameras, and Crisis has covered a lot of ground. In the first three chapters, our focus was retrospective. Chapter 1 provided a historical backdrop by placing BWCs in the larger context of technology's impact on policing over the past 150 years and by tracing the emergence of BWCs since the early 2000s. More specifically, over the past few decades, there has been growing reliance in policing on surveillance technologies, from dashboard in-car cameras and smartphones to CCTV and license plate readers. BWCs are the latest iteration of surveillance technology designed to enhance police practices. The adoption of BWCs since 2014 has been nothing short of remarkable. As the popularity of BWCs has grown rapidly, so too has the evidence base. New studies of BWCs seem to be published every week, and it is very difficult to keep up with the latest research on the technology. Moreover, the findings from some studies have been inconsistent and, in some cases, contradictory. In chapter 2, we reviewed the available evidence on the major claims made regarding the benefits of BWCs. We acknowledge that additional research has probably come out since this book has gone to print, so we may not have captured all published studies. Although more research is needed in a number of areas, our assessment of the evidence on several key outcomes is positive. For example, the majority of studies show that BWCs lead to reductions in citizen complaints against officers. Results from studies testing the impact of BWCs on officer use of force are less consistent, but on the whole, they suggest that cameras can lead to reductions in this important outcome. The research on officer perceptions, citizen perceptions, and evidentiary value is also positive. There has only been one cost-benefit study conducted to date, but the results showed sizable cost savings—on the order of $4 million per year. In sum, many of the claims made about BWCs are supported by the available evidence.

In chapter 3, we delved into the major concerns about BWCs, from citizen privacy and cost to the potential for unintended effects of officer discretion and proactivity. These are not small issues, and the takeaway message from chapter 3 is that BWCs programs are not easy to implement and manage. BWCs require an enormous investment in resources, and they touch nearly every aspect of police department operations. BWCs also have significant implications for numerous stakeholders outside the police department, from citizens and business owners to schools, hospitals, and downstream criminal justice actors. It is clear that if a police department hopes to experience any of the benefits described in chapter 2, it must successfully deal with the issues described in chapter 3.

In chapter 4, we took a step back and tried to understand the trends in BWC adoption. Given the complexities described in chapter 3, why have BWCs spread so quickly in policing? How have departments addressed the complexities that threaten to impede adoption? Will BWCs continue to diffuse in the future? We applied the diffusion of innovation and evidence-based policing frameworks to explore these questions. These frameworks provide an informed perspective on the how and why of the current state of affairs with BWCs in policing. Moreover, both frameworks predict continued adoption of BWCs in the years to come.

In chapter 5, we have explored three emerging challenges that departments will need to address in order to maintain the viability of their BWC program. Other challenges will undoubtedly emerge. Regardless of those challenges, we believe that adherence to the DOJ planning and implementation principles will provide the requisite foundation to successfully navigate new and emerging issues involving police BWCs. In this last section, we want to offer a few final thoughts on the future for BWCs in policing.

Police BWCs Are Here to Stay

The rate of BWC adoption has matched or exceeded the diffusion of other technologies, both in policing and generally. Arnulf Grubler has noted that most innovations take from fifteen to thirty years to achieve a 90 percent saturation level.[94] David Klinger has estimated that SWAT teams in policing achieved a 90 percent saturation level after approximately twenty-five years.[95] Michael White has estimated that the TASER less-lethal device achieved 75 percent diffusion within twelve years and 90 percent saturation by fifteen years.[96] BWCs, as we know them, have been around for approximately thirteen years. The first eight years of that history (2005–13) were characterized by a slow-growing interest in the technology. One-third of surveyed agencies (about thirty-nine hundred agencies) indicated that they had deployed BWCs to at least some of their officers by 2013.[97] But as we have stated previously, everything changed after the summer of 2014. In fall 2018, the Bureau of Justice Statistics released survey data from 2016, indicating that approximately half of all law enforcement agencies (47 percent) had deployed BWCs, including 80 percent of large agencies. That percentage has undoubtedly grown considerably since 2016.

BWCs emerged in a perfect storm of events that continue to drive their diffusion in policing. BWCs are inextricably linked to the crisis in police-community relations that emerged in 2014, both as a mechanism for enhancing transparency and community satisfaction and as a tool for boosting police accountability and evidence for prosecution. As such, the technology was almost immediately embraced by advocacy and civil rights groups, by the federal government, by police leadership groups, and by police officers themselves. The reasons for supporting BWCs no doubt varied across these key stakeholder groups, but the unifying theme centers on acceptance of the technology for the betterment of the policing profession.

This perfect storm has continued through 2018 and into 2019. The ubiquity of cameras in our society has spread at an unparalleled pace, forcing police to deploy cameras to keep up and to capture their side of the story. Unfortunately, controversial incidents have continued to occur, and many of these incidents highlight the value of police BWCs, either because a BWC captures the encounter (e.g., the response after the Las Vegas mass shooting in October 2017)[98] or because the officer did not have a BWC and now there is demand for that department to adopt them (e.g., US Border Patrol shooting of Claudia Gomez Gonzalez in June 2018).[99] Also, numerous incidents have demonstrated the value of police BWCs either as an accountability tool that captures police misconduct (e.g., the Detroit officer who physically beat a woman in a hospital in August 2018)[100] or as a protection against false claims made against officers by citizens (e.g., a Texas state trooper who was accused of sexual assault in May 2018).[101] Finally, advocates of the technology have made bold claims about the impact of BWCs, and in many cases, the evidence base suggests that those claims have merit. Police BWCs can positively influence several critically important outcomes for the police. In simple terms, police BWCs are here to stay.

Police BWCs Have Limitations

We have tried to emphasize throughout this book that BWCs have limitations. BWCs are not a silver bullet that will solve all of a police department's problems. BWCs are a tool—a useful tool for sure, based on the evidence presented in chapters 2 and 3. But they are just a tool. They cannot single-handedly repair decades of tension between police and citizens. They cannot eliminate bad policing. They cannot not provide movie-quality video and audio of every single police-citizen encounter. Seth Stoughton makes this point effectively with a comparison between BWCs and hammers (see Box 5.3). For some tasks, such as generating evidence or reducing citizen complaints, BWCs are appropriate and effective. For other tasks, such as enhancing police legitimacy and reducing use of force by officers, BWCs may be useful, but there are also alternative and perhaps more effective ways to accomplish those tasks. And for some tasks, like repairing decades of antagonism between police and a minority community, BWCs are ill suited for the job.

BOX 5.3

"Body-worn cameras are a tool. Tools should be used to accomplish normatively desirable tasks when they are an efficient way of accomplishing or facilitating that task. Following that logic, tools should not be used when the task itself is inappropriate or when the tool is ill-suited for the job at hand. To make this point more directly, consider that most indelicate of tools: the hammer. For some tasks, such as putting in nails, the hammer is among the best tools to use. For other tasks, such as extracting nails, the hammer is a perfectly reasonable option even though other tools, such as a nail puller or cat's paw crowbar, may prove marginally more efficacious. For some tasks, such as cleaning a windshield, using a hammer will not only be ineffective, it may prove destructively counterproductive. And some tasks, like bashing in another's head, are themselves so objectionable that a hammer should not be used even if its use would easily accomplish the task."
—Seth Stoughton, "Police Body-Worn Cameras"

Beyond the "right tool for the right job" analogy, there is also the potential for human and technological error. The officer may fail to activate the BWC, either intentionally or unintentionally. Police-citizen encounters are very fluid and can escalate from an informal conversation to a life-or-death situation in seconds. The officer may activate the BWC but not until after critical events have occurred and the officer's safety (and the safety of others) is no longer in jeopardy. Also, the BWC may fail to provide definitive audio and video evidence of what transpired. The view from the camera may be obstructed by the officer's "shooting platform." Or perhaps the officer may see or feel something that cannot be captured on a forward-facing BWC (e.g., a suspect tensing up; something to the side in the officer's peripheral vision). BWC footage during a struggle or foot pursuit can be unwatchable, and even audio can become muffled. In plain terms, this is not *Live PD* or *COPS*. BWCs have limitations, both human and technological. We must be realistic about what BWCs can and cannot do. Otherwise, the false narrative surrounding the technology will lead to disappointment and misconceptions and may actually do more harm than good.

Given the aforementioned limitations of BWCs, police departments should continue to focus on evidence-based practices that can facilitate the achievement of their core responsibilities. There are numerous tools and strategies with an established evidence base supporting their positive impact, such as crime analysis, problem-oriented policing, hot spots policing, and targeted offender strategies (e.g., focused deterrence).[102] Police departments should also seek to achieve police legitimacy through procedurally just treatment of citizens.[103] Each police-citizen encounter every single day represents an opportunity to engage in procedural justice and to improve citizens' perceptions of the police. The available research strongly suggests that enhanced police legitimacy will lead to greater levels of citizen cooperation and compliance with the law, both of which are central to the police mission.[104]

Police chiefs do not have to go it alone in their search for evidence-based practices. There are public directories of evidence-based practices, most notably CrimeSolutions.gov, the George Mason University Evidence-Based Policing Matrix, and resources from the United Kingdom College of Policing.[105] There are also practitioner-based organizations focused on the identification and dissemination of evidence-based practices, such as the Police Executive Research Forum, the Police Foundation, the American Society of Evidence-Based Policing, and the Society of Evidence-Based Policing.[106] In sum, BWCs are a twenty-first-century policing tool with a growing evidence base, but they are not the only (or even best) answer to problems that have plagued police for decades (e.g., police–minority community relations). BWCs should serve as one piece in a larger mosaic of twenty-first-century evidence-based policing practices.

Research on BWCs Will Continue to Generate Mixed Findings

We believe that mixed findings will be the continuing story that emerges from BWC research. There are a few reasons for this. First, there are no absolutes. What program or strategy is effective 100 percent of the time? Medications that are approved by the US Federal Drug Administration rarely cure every single human afflicted with a disease or ailment, and many medications produce a host of unintended side effects. It is not unheard of for someone to get the flu *after* getting a flu shot. In some cases, the description of potential side effects to a medication in a television ad takes as long to recite as the rest of the commercial itself. Programming in criminal justice is no different. Programs that are considered evidence based, such as hot spots policing, are not foolproof. Why should we expect any different with police BWCs?

Moreover, researchers may view the body of available evidence differently. Though we certainly acknowledge the mixed evidence, we take a decidedly optimistic view about the research on BWCs. John Maskaly and colleagues and Aili Malm do the same.[107] However, Cynthia Lum and colleagues come to a much more skeptical conclusion: "BWCs have not had statistically significant or consistent effects on most measures of officer and citizen behavior or citizens' views of police. . . . Overall, then perhaps anticipated effects from BWCs have been overestimated."[108] In simple term, mixed findings may also lead to varying assessments of the strength of the evidence.

In fact, there is probably a greater likelihood of mixed findings with police BWCs for the reasons we have described throughout this book. BWCs come with an extremely high degree of difficulty. They require an enormous investment in money and resources, and they touch nearly every aspect of a police department's operations. Integration and acceptance of the technology among officers and key external stakeholders are not guaranteed. The deployment of police BWCs brings into play numerous weighty issues, from citizen privacy and the recording of vulnerable populations to data security and technological infrastructure requirements. And there is often significant external pressure to deploy the cameras quickly without proper planning and collaborative engagement.

Moreover, we have made the case that an organization's pre-BWC starting point makes a difference. Why is the organization deploying cameras? Has it just experienced a scandal? Are BWCs ordered by a federal court as a remedy to overcome a "pattern or practice" of unconstitutional policing?[109] Is the chief deploying cameras to defuse community tension after a controversial critical incident? Or is the department deploying cameras as part of its continuing efforts to ensure professional, evidence-based policing? Moreover, did the department go through the proper planning and implementation to avoid the traditional pitfalls of BWC implementation failure? As we have said previously, there are eighteen thousand law enforcement agencies in the United States, and though there will not be eighteen thousand different BWC stories, there are bound to be many. Some of those stories will be like Rialto's. Some will be like Washington, DC's. And most will probably be somewhere in between.

Next Steps for BWC Research

To reconcile the varied results, the future of BWC research should include a more thorough, and more standardized, approach to documenting implementation, organizational culture, technical support, and front-line motivations. Ideally, we would want to implement BWCs in numerous departments and retain a standardized set of metrics to evaluate these variables. The literature is, however, dominated by studies in individual departments. To overcome this challenge, researchers could start to agree on some universal metrics, so that the plethora of individual case studies from single departments could be better coalesced into a wider research framework, fulfilling the role usually performed by a multilevel study. To date, there are too many different outcomes measured in different ways in different individual departments, with too little agreement as to the critical dependent and independent variables. In the future, individual agency studies will have to make a less idiosyncratic contribution to the BWC canon.

There Is Help—Use It

BWCs are far from easy. This is one of the most important takeaways of *Cops, Cameras, and Crisis*, and at the risk of beating a dead horse, it bears repeating one last time. Buying cameras and outfitting officers is the easiest part with this technology. But the groundwork that must be laid beforehand is substantial. And the requirements to successfully manage the BWC program after deployment are just as substantial. As we said in chapter 1, the costs are high, the stakes are high, and the degree of difficulty is high. If BWCs are to generate positive impacts, a department must make a long-term, deep commitment. The department must be transparent, collaborative, flexible, and informed. It must also be vigilant and forward thinking. These are terms that do not typically come to mind when describing a police department. In fact, Dorothy Guyot's well-used description of the difficulty of making change in a police department—she equates it to "bending granite"—is still painfully appropriate for many police departments in the twenty-first century.[110] There is good news, however. The good news is that there is a wide and continually growing community of support for departments that are planning, implementing, or managing existing BWC programs. Our description of the "societal entity of innovators and their social networks" in chapter 4 highlights the supports within the policing profession with regard to this technology. Leadership and professional organizations, such as the International Association of Chiefs of Police, the Police Foundation, and the Police Executive Research Forum (among others), provide a wealth of information on police BWCs. The research community is also an important source of support, and not just for evaluating a BWC program. Police departments should collaborate with researchers and academics from local universities to draw on their expertise.

Last, the federal government committed very early on to the diffusion of police BWCs, and the Department of Justice provides a wide array of resources—financial and otherwise—to facilitate the deployment of police BWCs. The Obama administration's early commitment to BWCs was grounded in their potential to improve police-community relations. Much has changed under the Trump administration (a mild understatement to say the least!). It is notable that the federal government's investment in BWCs has not. Perhaps the rationale for that investment has changed (less about police-community relations and more now about evidentiary value and officer safety), but the investment is still there. The support is still there. The resources are still there. Those resources serve as the foundation for much of this book, and departments should take advantage of what is out there for guidance, information, and technical assistance. The requirements to successfully deploy police BWCs are steep, and the available conventional and evidentiary wisdom on the technology can both ease the burden and lessen the potential for implementation failure. In the end, BWCs are a tool, but they are an important tool. And they can be the right tool for helping police achieve a range of critically important objectives tied to their core mission.

NOTES

CHAPTER 1. SETTING THE STAGE

1. Walker and Katz, *Police in America*.
2. Goldstein, "Improving Policing"; White and Fradella, *Stop and Frisk*.
3. National Institute of Justice, "Law Enforcement"; Center for Evidence-Based Crime Policy, "Evidence-Based Policing Matrix."
4. American Society of Evidence-Based Policing, home page; Society of Evidence-Based Policing, home page.
5. Lussenhop, "Police Geeks."
6. Pilant, "Spotlight on In-Car Video Systems."
7. International Association of Chiefs of Police, *Impact of Video Evidence*.
8. Reaves, *Local Police Departments, 2013*.
9. Ratcliffe, *Video Surveillance*; Welsh and Farrington, "Public Area CCTV."
10. Erpenbach "Whole World Is Watching"; Harris, "Picture This."
11. See also the ACLU's smartphone app for recording encounters with police, called "Police Tape." ACLU New Jersey, "ACLU-NJ Launches." Consequently, many police leaders instruct their officers to always assume that their actions are being recorded.
12. Flight, "Black Box," 1.
13. Goodall, *Guidance*.
14. White, *Police Officer Body-Worn Cameras*.
15. *Floyd v. City of New York*, 959 F. Supp. 2d 540 (2013).
16. Miller, Toliver, and Police Executive Research Forum, *Implementing a Body-Worn Camera Program*.
17. White, *Police Officer Body-Worn Cameras*.
18. Reaves, *Local Police Departments, 2013*, 4.
19. Hudson, "Building Trust."
20. Dann and Rafferty, "Obama Requests."
21. President's Task Force on 21st Century Policing, *Final Report of the President's Task Force*, 1.
22. Major Cities Chiefs and Major County Sheriffs Associations, *Survey of Technology Needs*.
23. Police Executive Research Forum, *Costs and Benefits*, 9.
24. Hyland, *Body-Worn Cameras*.
25. International Association of Chiefs of Police, "Body-Worn Cameras."

26. Stanley, *Police Body-Mounted Cameras.*
27. Bureau of Justice Assistance, "Fraternal Order of Police."
28. Sousa, Miethe, and Sakiyama, "Inconsistencies in Public Opinion"; White, Todak, and Gaub, "Assessing Citizen Perceptions."
29. Body-Worn Camera: Training and Technical Assistance, "About Us."
30. Bureau of Justice Assistance, "Toolkit."
31. Body-Worn Camera: Training and Technical Assistance, "What You Need to Know."
32. Bureau of Justice Assistance, "Checklist"; Body-Worn Camera: Training and Technical Assistance, "Policy Review Scorecard."
33. Police Executive Research Forum, *Costs and Benefits*, 9.
34. White, *Police Officer Body-Worn Cameras.*
35. Lum et al., *Existing and Ongoing Body Worn Camera Research.*
36. Lum et al., "Research on Body-Worn Cameras."
37. Farrar, *Self-Awareness to Being Watched.*
38. Mesa Police Department, *On-Officer Body Camera System.*
39. Katz et al., *Evaluating the Impact.*
40. Jennings, Lynch, and Fridell, "Evaluating the Impact."
41. White, Gaub, and Todak, "To Record or Not to Record?"
42. Jennings, Fridell, and Lynch, "Cops and Cameras."
43. Braga et al., "Effects of Body-Worn Cameras."
44. Ellis, Jenkins, and Smith, *Evaluation.*
45. Morrow, Katz, and Choate, "Assessing the Impact"; Owens, Mann, and McKenna, *Essex Body Worn Video Trial.*
46. White, Todak, and Gaub, "Assessing Citizen Perceptions," 699.
47. Officer support: Gaub et al., "Officer Perceptions"; Jennings, Fridell, and Lynch, "Cops and Cameras." Citizen support: Crow et al., "Community Perceptions"; Sousa, Miethe, and Sakiyama, "Inconsistencies in Public Opinion."
48. Braga et al., *Benefits of Body-Worn Cameras.*
49. Edmonton Police Service, *Body Worn Video*; and Grossmith et al., *Police, Camera, Evidence.*
50. Yokum, Ravishankar, and Coppock, *Evaluating the Effects.*
51. Ariel et al., "Wearing Body Cameras."
52. Levenson and Allen, "Boston Police Union."
53. Berman, "After Justine Damond Shooting."
54. Lillis and Chavez, "Cops Muted Their Body Cams."
55. Wallace et al., "Camera-Induced Passivity."
56. Braga et al., "Effects of Body-Worn Cameras," 538.
57. Sutherland et al., "Post-Experimental Follow-Ups."
58. KTLA, "Local Police Officers Accused"; Dulaney, "Rialto Police Sex Scandal."
59. White, Todak, and Gaub, "Integration and Acceptance."
60. Hollinshed, "Ferguson Police."

61. Rogers, *Diffusion of Innovations*.
62. Wejnert, "Integrating Models."
63. Sagan, *Billions and Billions*, 190.
64. United Kingdom College of Policing, "What Is Evidence-Based Policing?"
65. Miller and Miller, "Rethinking Program Fidelity"; Pew Charitable Trusts, "Implementation Oversight"; White, *Police Officer Body-Worn Cameras*.

CHAPTER 2. ARE BODY-WORN CAMERAS
A "SILVER BULLET" SOLUTION?

1. Lum et al., *Existing and Ongoing Body Worn Camera Research*; Lum et al., "Research on Body-Worn Cameras"; Maskaly et al., "Effects of Body-Worn Cameras"; and White, *Police Officer Body-Worn Cameras*.
2. Tyler, *Why People Obey the Law*, 375.
3. Tyler, "Psychological Perspectives."
4. Tyler, *Why People Obey the Law*; Tyler and Huo, *Trust in the Law*.
5. Sunshine and Tyler, "Role of Procedural Justice."
6. Tyler and Huo, *Trust in the Law*.
7. Mazerolle et al., "Shaping Citizen Perceptions"; Sunshine and Tyler, "Role of Procedural Justice"; Tyler and Fagan, "Legitimacy and Cooperation"; White, Mulvey, and Dario, "Arrestees and Their Perceptions."
8. Police Executive Research Forum, *Costs and Benefits*.
9. Braga et al., "Effects of Body-Worn Cameras."
10. Pelfrey and Keener, "Police Body Worn Cameras."
11. Mesa Police Department, *On-Officer Body Camera System*; Ready and Young, "On-Officer Video Cameras"; Roy, "On-Officer Video Cameras."
12. Mesa Police Department, *On-Officer Body Camera System*.
13. Headley, Guerette, and Shariati, "Field Experiment."
14. Sousa, Miethe, and Sakiyama, "Inconsistencies in Public Opinion."
15. Wallace et al., "Camera-Induced Passivity."
16. Gillet et al., "Perceived Organizational Support."
17. Kyle and White, "Impact of Law Enforcement Officer Perceptions."
18. Wallace et al., "Camera-Induced Passivity."
19. Walker, "Police Accountability," 26.
20. Crow et al., "Community Perceptions."
21. Lum et al., "Research on Body-Worn Cameras," 106.
22. Tyler and Wakslak, "Profiling and Police Legitimacy."
23. Culhane, Boman, and Schweitzer, "Public Perceptions."
24. Ibid.
25. Tyler, "Psychological Perspectives"; Tyler and Fagan, "Legitimacy and Cooperation"; Tyler and Huo, *Trust in the Law*; Tyler, Goff, and MacCoun, "Impact of Psychological Science."
26. Sherman et al., *Preventing Crime*.

27. Hamm et al., "Do Body-Worn Cameras Reduce Eyewitness Cooperation with the Police?"

28. Grossmith et al., *Police, Camera, Evidence.*

29. White, Todak, and Gaub, "Integration and Acceptance."

30. White, *Police Officer Body-Worn Cameras.*

31. Sousa, Miethe, and Sakiyama, "Inconsistencies in Public Opinion"; and White, Todak, and Gaub, "Integration and Acceptance."

32. White, Todak, and Gaub, "Assessing Citizen Perceptions."

33. Gaub et al., "Officer Perceptions"; and White, Todak, and Gaub, "Integration and Acceptance."

34. Farrar, *Self-Awareness to Being Watched*; Munger and Harris, "Effects of an Observer"; Van Rompay, Vonk, and Fransen, "Eye of the Camera"; and Wahl et al., "Red Light Cameras."

35. Farrar, *Self-Awareness to Being Watched*, 8.

36. Ariel, Farrar, and Sutherland, "Effect of Police Body-Worn Cameras."

37. Sutherland et al., "Post-Experimental Follow-Ups," 114.

38. Flight, "Black Box," 5.

39. Maskaly et al., "Effects of Body-Worn Cameras," 682.

40. Lum et al., "Research on Body-Worn Cameras," 101.

41. For the full directory, see White, Gaub, and Padilla, "Impact of BWCs on Use of Force."

42. Farrar, *Self-Awareness to Being Watched*; Ariel, Farrar, and Sutherland, "Effect of Police Body-Worn Cameras."

43. Sutherland et al., "Post-Experimental Follow-Ups."

44. Flight, "Black Box"; Maskaly et al., "Effects of Body-Worn Cameras."

45. Flight, "Black Box," 5.

46. Lum et al., "Research on Body-Worn Cameras," 99.

47. For the full directory, see White, Gaub, and Padilla, "Impact of BWCs on Citizen Complaints."

48. White and Coldren, "Body-Worn Cameras."

49. Winton, "2 Rialto Police Officers Resign."

50. The form and function of Collaborative Reform has changed considerably under the Trump administration. COPS, "Collaborative Reform Initiative."

51. Yokum et al., *Evaluating the Effects*, 20.

52. Todak, Gaub, and White, "Importance of External Stakeholders"; and White, *Police Officer Body-Worn Cameras.*

53. Hollinshed, "Ferguson Police."

54. White, Todak, and Gaub, "Integration and Acceptance."

55. McClure et al., *Perceptions of Police.*

56. Katz et al., *Evaluating the Impact.*

57. Hedberg, Katz, and Choate, "Body-Worn Cameras," 642.

58. Yokum et al., *Evaluating the Effects.*

59. Braga et al., *Benefits of Body-Worn Cameras*.
60. Wallace et al., "Camera-Induced Passivity."
61. Ariel, Sutherland, and Sherman, "Preventing Treatment Spillover," 13.
62. Ibid.
63. We thank an anonymous peer reviewer for raising this point.
64. Ariel et al., "Contagious Accountability," 307.
65. Police Executive Research Forum, *Costs and Benefits*, 9.
66. Katz et al., *Evaluating the Impact*.
67. Braga et al., *Benefits of Body-Worn Cameras*.
68. Merola et al., *Body Worn Cameras and the Courts*.
69. Ellis, Jenkins, and Smith, *Isle of Wight*; Goodall, *Guidance*; ODS Consulting, *Body Worn Video Projects*.
70. Miller, Toliver, and Police Executive Research Forum, *Implementing a Body-Worn Camera Program*; White, *Police Officer Body-Worn Cameras*.
71. Owens, Mann, and McKenna, *Essex Body Worn Video Trial*.
72. Morrow, Katz, and Choate, "Assessing the Impact"; and Katz et al., *Evaluating the Impact*.
73. Yokum et al., *Evaluating the Effects*.
74. White et al., "Implicate or Exonerate."
75. Lum et al., "Research on Body-Worn Cameras," 108.
76. National Institute of Justice, "Sentinel Events Initiative."
77. Wood, "Police Could Be Doing So Much More."
78. Phelps et al., "Experiential Learning."
79. Koen, Willis, and Mastrofski, "Effects of Body-Worn Cameras."
80. Toronto Police Service, *Body-Worn Cameras*.

CHAPTER 3. THE CHALLENGES AND LIMITATIONS OF BODY-WORN CAMERAS

1. Del Pozo, "Body Cameras and Policy."
2. Marlow and Stanley, "Police Body Camera Recommendations."
3. Crow et al., "Community Perceptions."
4. Grossmith et al., *Police, Camera, Evidence*.
5. Toronto Police Service, *Body-Worn Cameras*.
6. Edmonton Police Service, *Body Worn Video*.
7. Taylor et al., "Police Detainee Perspectives."
8. Edmonton Police Service, *Body Worn Video*.
9. Toronto Police Service, *Body-Worn Cameras*.
10. Grossmith et al., *Police, Camera, Evidence*.
11. Crow et al., "Community Perceptions."
12. White, *Police Officer Body-Worn Cameras*; Stanley, *Police Body-Mounted Cameras*.
13. Toronto Police Service, *Body-Worn Cameras*.
14. Goodison and Wilson, *Citizen Perceptions*, 58.

15. Miller, Toliver, and Police Executive Research Forum, *Implementing a Body-Worn Camera Program*; White, *Police Officer Body-Worn Cameras*.
16. White, Flippin, and Katz, *Policy and Practice*.
17. Miller, Toliver, and Police Executive Research Forum, *Implementing a Body-Worn Camera Program*; Stanley, *Police Body-Mounted Cameras*.
18. White, *Police Officer Body-Worn Cameras*.
19. Ibid.
20. Lum et al., "Research on Body-Worn Cameras," 106.
21. Toronto Police Service, *Body-Worn Cameras*.
22. Braga et al., "Effects of Body-Worn Cameras," 521.
23. Lum, Koper, and Willis, "Understanding the Limits"; Manning, *Technology of Policing*.
24. White, Flippin, Katz, *Policy and Practice*, 9.
25. Ibid.
26. Gaub, Todak, and White, "One Size Doesn't Fit All," 2.
27. Ibid.
28. Ibid., 14.
29. Williams and Moyer, "One Month after D.C. Police Shooting."
30. White, Flippin, Katz, *Policy and Practice*.
31. Lillis and Chavez, "Cops Muted Their Body Cams."
32. White, Flippin, Katz, *Policy and Practice*, 11.
33. Ibid.
34. Ibid., 11.
35. McClure et al., *Perceptions of Police*.
36. White, Flippin, Katz, *Policy and Practice*, 13.
37. Ibid.
38. Ibid.
39. Ibid.
40. Ibid.
41. Ibid.
42. Ibid., 17.
43. Rushin and Edwards, "De-policing."
44. Lichtblau, "F.B.I. Director Says."
45. MacDonald, *War on Cops*, 1.
46. See Maguire, Nix, and Campbell, "War on Cops"; and Pyrooz et al., "Was There a Ferguson Effect."
47. Shjarback et al., "De-policing and Crime"; see also Morgan and Pally, *Ferguson, Gray, and Davis*.
48. De Vries and van Gelder, "Explaining Workplace Delinquency"; and Martin, Wellen, and Grimmer, "Eye on Your Work."
49. Stanley, *Police Body-Mounted Cameras*.
50. Ariel et al., "Paradoxical Effects."

51. Ibid., 1.
52. Manning, "Police Mandate."
53. Ohlin, "President's Commission," 106.
54. Ariel et al., "Paradoxical Effects."
55. Gaub et al., "Officer Perceptions."
56. Sherman et al., *Preventing Crime*.
57. Katz et al., *Evaluating the Impact*.
58. Hedberg, Katz, and Choate, "Body-Worn Cameras."
59. Ready and Young, "On-Officer Video Cameras," 454.
60. Braga et al., "Effects of Body-Worn Cameras."
61. McClure et al., *Perceptions of Police*; Ariel, "Police Body Cameras"; Headley, Guerette, and Shariati, "Field Experiment."
62. Grossmith et al., *Police, Camera, Evidence*, 1.
63. Yokum et al., *Evaluating the Effects*.
64. Ready and Young, "On-Officer Video Cameras."; Hedberg, Katz, and Choate ("Body-Worn Cameras") note that Ready and Young failed to control for the interaction between volunteer status and the treatment effect (the study involved both volunteers and officers required to wear a BWC). Hedberg, Katz, and Choate reran their analyses and stated, "If there are differences between the volunteers and non-volunteers, then the paper only plausibly reflects the impact of the non-volunteers" ("Body-Worn Cameras," 7).
65. Peterson et al., *Milwaukee Police Department's Body-Worn Camera Program*, 7.
66. Wallace et al., "Camera-Induced Passivity."
67. Ibid.
68. Goodall, *Guidance*; Katz et al., *Evaluating the Impact*; Toronto Police Service *Body-Worn Cameras*; Braga et al., "Effects of Body-Worn Cameras."
69. Ariel, "Police Body Cameras"; Headley, Guerette, and Shariati, "Field Experiment"; McClure et al., *Perceptions of Police*; Ready and Young, "On-Officer Video Cameras."
70. Grossmith et al., *Police, Camera, Evidence*; Hedberg, Katz, and Choate, "Body-Worn Cameras"; Yokum et al., *Evaluating the Effects*; Peterson et al., *Milwaukee Police Department's Body-Worn Camera Program*; Wallace et al., "Camera-Induced Passivity."
71. Ready and Young, "On-Officer Video Cameras"; Headley, Guerette, and Shariati, "Field Experiment"; Braga et al., "Effects of Body-Worn Cameras."
72. Toronto Police Service, *Body-Worn Cameras*.
73. Braga et al., "Effects of Body-Worn Cameras," 538.
74. Nowacki and Willits, "Adoption of Body Cameras."
75. White, *Police Officer Body-Worn Cameras*.
76. See Ariel et al., "Wearing Body Cameras"; Levenson and Allen, "Boston Police Union."
77. Headley, Guerette, and Shariati, "Field Experiment."

78. Braga et al., *Benefits of Body-Worn Cameras*.
79. Katz et al., *Evaluating the Impact*; Kyle and White, "Impact of Law Enforcement Officer Perceptions"; Wallace et al., "Camera-Induced Passivity."
80. Todak, Gaub, and White, "Importance of External Stakeholders."
81. Ibid.
82. Ibid.
83. Ibid.
84. Ibid.

CHAPTER 4. UNDERSTANDING BODY-WORN CAMERA ADOPTION

1. Ariel, Farrar, and Sutherland, "Effect of Police Body-Worn Cameras"; Edmonton Police Service, *Body Worn Video*; Farrar *Self-Awareness to Being Watched*; Goodall, *Guidance*; Laur et al., *Proof of Concept Study*.
2. Reaves, *Local Police Departments, 2013*.
3. Major Cities Chiefs and Major County Sheriffs Associations, *Survey of Technology Needs*, ii.
4. United States Bureau of Justice Statistics, "Data Collection."
5. Hyland, *Body-Worn Cameras*.
6. Rogers, *Diffusion of Innovations*.
7. Wejnert, "Integrating Models."
8. Ibid.
9. Weisburd et al., "Reforming to Preserve."
10. Klinger, "Spreading Diffusion."
11. White, "Restraint and Technology."
12. Wejnert notes that innovations tend to have consequences that are either public or private, but in some cases, the consequences "are not so dichotomous" and may have significance among both private and public entities ("Integrating Models," 301). The TASER falls into this latter category.
13. Todak, Gaub, and White, "Importance of External Stakeholders," 457.
14. Ibid., 455–56.
15. White, Gaub, and Padilla, "Impacts of BWCs on Citizen Complaints."
16. White, Gaub, and Padilla, "Impacts of BWCs on Use of Force."
17. Morrow, Katz, and Choate, "Assessing the Impact"; Owens, Mann, and McKenna, *Essex Body Worn Video Trial*.
18. ODS Consulting, *Body Worn Video Projects*.
19. Katz et al., *Evaluating the Impact*.
20. Braga et al., *Benefits of Body-Worn Cameras*.
21. Stanley, *Police Body-Mounted Cameras*, 2.
22. Dunn and Lieberman, "Body Cameras Are Key." Though none of those incidents were captured on a police BWC, Dunn and Lieberman's point is well taken. There have been numerous cases where an officer-involved shooting was captured on

the officer's BWC (or that of a fellow officer), and the audio and video evidence is crucial to understanding what transpired during that encounter.

23. White, Todak, and Gaub, "Assessing Citizen Perceptions," 699.
24. Phillips, "Eyes are Not Cameras."
25. Braga et al., *Benefits of Body-Worn Cameras*.
26. Gaub et al., *Implementing a Police Body-Worn Camera Program*, 9.
27. Ariel et al., "Wearing Body Cameras Increases Assaults."
28. White, Todak, and Gaub, "Integration and Acceptance."
29. White, Todak, and Gaub, "Assessing Citizen Perceptions"; White, Todak, and Gaub, "Integration and Acceptance"; McClure et al., *Perceptions of Police*.
30. Katz et al., *Evaluating the Impact* (generally); Berman, "Minneapolis Police Shooting" (officer-involved shootings).
31. International Association of Chiefs of Police, "Deliberations."
32. Wallace et al., "Camera-Induced Passivity."
33. Braga et al., "Effects of Body-Worn Cameras."
34. Yant, "Officers Get Raise."
35. White, Todak, and Gaub, "Integration and Acceptance"; Bureau of Justice Assistance, "Checklist."
36. White, Todak, and Gaub, "Integration and Acceptance," 672.
37. Wejnert, "Integrating Models."
38. Eith and Durose, *Contacts between Police and the Public, 2008*.
39. International Association of Chiefs of Police, "Welcome to IACP 2019."
40. Major Cities Chiefs Association, "Conference Overview."
41. Center for Problem-Oriented Policing, "26th Annual Problem-Oriented Policing Conference."
42. President's Commission, *Task Force Report*.
43. California Commission, "POST Monthly Report."
44. California Commission, *POST Monthly Report*, 1.
45. Miller, Toliver, and Police Executive Research Forum, *Implementing a Body-Worn Camera Program*.
46. International Association of Chiefs of Police, "Body-Worn Cameras."
47. Fraternal Order of Police, home page.
48. Bureau of Justice Assistance, "Fraternal Order of Police."
49. Bureau of Justice Assistance, "Toolkit"; Body-Worn Camera: Training and Technical Assistance, "What You Need to Know."
50. Wejnert, "Integrating Models," 303.
51. Law Enforcement Executive Forum, home page; PoliceOne, home page; Police Policy Studies Council, home page.
52. Meadows, "Evanston Police."
53. Ripley, "Big Test."
54. Williams, "Minneapolis Officer Failed."
55. Williams et al., "Police Body Cameras."

56. Axon, home page.

57. Arizona Association of Chiefs of Police, "AACOP Sponsors."

58. VIEVU, home page; WatchGuard, home page; Motorola Solutions, "Police Body Cameras."

59. Police Foundation, "Body-Worn Camera Study."

60. Jennings, Fridell, and Lynch, "Cops and Cameras."

61. Gaub et al., "Officer Perceptions."

62. Wejnert, "Integrating Models."

63. Ibid., 305.

64. *Floyd v. City of New York*, 959 F. Supp. 2d 540 (S.D.N.Y. 2013).

65. Ready and Young, "On-Officer Video Cameras"; Katz et al., *Evaluating the Impact*.

66. Los Angeles Police Department, "LAPD Rolls Out First Cameras."

67. Wejnert, "Integrating Models," 310.

68. Hudson, "Building Trust."

69. President's Task Force on 21st Century Policing, *Final Report*.

70. James, "Nevada Likely to Become Second State."

71. Urban Institute, "Legislation Tracker."

72. Levenson and Allen, "Boston Police Union."

73. Hamilton, "Police Union Sues."

74. Johnson, "Judge Dismisses Mobile's Case."

75. Briscoe, "Judge Says CPD Violated State Labor Laws."

76. General population: Crow et al., "Community Perceptions"; Sousa, Miethe, and Sakiyama, "Inconsistencies in Public Opinion." Citizens with BWC-recorded encounters: White, Todak, and Gaub, "Assessing Citizen Perceptions."

77. White, Todak, and Gaub, "Integration and Acceptance."

78. Ibid.

79. McClure et al., *Perceptions of Police*.

80. Goodison and Wilson, *Citizen Perceptions*.

81. Ratcliffe, *Reducing Crime*, 185.

82. Ibid.

83. Ibid.

84. Miller, Toliver, and Police Executive Research Forum, *Implementing a Body-Worn Camera Program*.

85. Sherman et al., *Preventing Crime*.

86. United Kingdom College of Policing, "Welcome to the Crime Reduction Toolkit."

CHAPTER 5. CHARTING A COURSE FOR BODY-WORN CAMERAS IN THE TWENTY-FIRST CENTURY

1. Wolfe and Nix, "Police Officers' Trust" (morale); Wallace et al., "Camera-Induced Passivity" (proactivity).

2. White and Coldren, "Body-Worn Cameras."

3. Todak, Gaub, and White, "Importance of External Stakeholders."

4. Berman, "After Justine Damond Shooting."

5. Ariel et al., "Report."

6. Hedberg, Katz, and Choate, "Body-Worn Cameras," 642.

7. Katz et al., *Evaluating the Impact*.

8. The New Orleans Police Department monitors BWC activation compliance as part of its federal consent decree, and it routinely reports compliance near 100 percent. The high activation compliance is, no doubt, tied to the pressure placed on officers to meet the standards set by the federal monitor and judge. In fact, for some time, a documented failure to activate resulted in an officer receiving an unpaid day off. More recently, the department has moved to a "three strikes" rule, whereby the unpaid day off is the discipline for a third failure to activate (in a calendar year).

9. Mitchell, *2014 Annual Report*.

10. Mesa Police Department, *On-Officer Body Camera System*.

11. McClure et al., *Perceptions of Police*; White, Gaub, and Todak, "To Record or Not to Record?"

12. Lawrence et al., "Activation of Body-Worn Cameras."

13. Walker and Archbold, *New World*.

14. White and Fradella, *Stop and Frisk*.

15. White, Flippin, and Katz, *Policy and Practice*.

16. Alpert and McLean, "Where Is the Goal Line?"

17. Diaz-Zuniga, "New Bodycams Start Recording"; Anthony, "New Holster."

18. For a discussion of the CSI effect, see Shelton, *"CSI Effect."*

19. Hannaford-Agor, "New CSI Effect?"

20. Gaub, Todak, and White, "One Size Doesn't Fit All."

21. White and Coldren, "Body-Worn Cameras."

22. See Gaub, Todak, and White, "One Size Doesn't Fit All."

23. Boivin et al., "Perspective Bias"; and Phillips, "Eyes Are Not Cameras."

24. Gaub, Todak, and White, "One Size Doesn't Fit All"; Todak, Gaub, and White, "Importance of External Stakeholders."

25. Knibbs, "Seattle Police."

26. Urban Institute, "Legislation Tracker."

27. Binker, "New NC Body Camera Law."

28. Las Vegas Metropolitan Police Department, "Body Worn Camera Recordings."

29. Fjardo, "LAPD Body Cam Footage."

30. Seattle Police Department, "1.115—Media Release."

31. Associated Press, "LAPD Releases First Body Cam Footage."

32. GbMb, "PB to TB Conversion."

33. Hu, "Metadata Collection," 1427.

34. Swire and Woo, "Privacy and Cybersecurity Lessons," 1477.

35. Newman, "Police Bodycams Can Be Hacked."

36. Ibid.

37. Swire and Woo, "Privacy and Cybersecurity Lessons."
38. Hu, "Metadata Collection," 1428.
39. Pegues, "Increasing Use."
40. Hu, "Metadata Collection."
41. Ibid., 1443.
42. Ibid.
43. Introna and Nissenbaum, "Facial Recognition Technology."
44. Woodward et al., *Biometrics*, 12.
45. Bowman, "Tampa Drops Face-Recognition Technology System."
46. Murphy and Bray, "Face Recognition Devices Failed."
47. Metz and Singer, "Newspaper Shooting."
48. Harwell, "Facial Recognition May Be Coming."
49. Leadership Conference, "Letter to Axon."
50. Singer, "Amazon's Facial Recognition."
51. Gershgorn, "America's Biggest Body-Camera Company."
52. Kawamoto, "If Facial Recognition Comes."
53. Ibid.
54. Bureau of Justice Assistance, "Toolkit."
55. Bureau of Justice Assistance, "Body-Worn Cameras."
56. Gaub, Todak, and White, "One Size Doesn't Fit All."
57. CNA: Analysis & Solutions, "Safety and Security"; ASU Center for Violence Prevention and Community Safety, "Training and Technical Assistance"; Justice and Security Strategies, home page.
58. Body-Worn Camera: Training and Technical Assistance, "What You Need to Know."
59. Body-Worn Camera: Training and Technical Assistance, "Body-Worn Camera Resources."
60. Bureau of Justice Assistance, "Toolkit."
61. Bureau of Justice Assistance, "Checklist."
62. Cissner and Farole, *Avoiding Failures*; Miller and Miller, "Rethinking Program Fidelity"; Pew Charitable Trusts, "Implementation Oversight."
63. Reuland, *Guide*; Sadd and Grinc, *Policing*.
64. Nored, Carlan, and Goodman, "Incentives and Obstacles"; and Pretrial Justice Institute, "Pretrial Services Program Implementation."
65. Reno et al., *Critical Elements*.
66. See also Miller, Toliver, and Police Executive Research Forum, *Implementing a Body-Worn Camera Program*.
67. Bureau of Justice Assistance, "Checklist."
68. Alpert and McLean, "Where Is the Goal Line?," 681.
69. Bureau of Justice Assistance, "Checklist."
70. Smaller agencies may not have all of the aforementioned units.
71. See, for example, Nix and Wolfe, "Sensitivity to the Ferguson Effect."

72. Bureau of Justice Assistance, "Checklist.

73. Fyfe, "Police Use of Deadly Force"; and White, "Controlling Police Decisions."

74. Terrill and Paoline, "Police Use of Less Lethal Force."

75. Alpert, Kenney, and Dunham, "Police Pursuits and the Use of Force."

76. Bobb, *13th Semiannual Report.*

77. Walker and Archbold, *New World.*

78. White, *Current Issues and Controversies.*

79. Body-Worn Camera: Training and Technical Assistance, "Scorecard."

80. The PIP Policy Review Scorecard is not prescriptive or directional; it only assesses comprehensiveness (e.g., is a specific issue covered in policy?). BJA believes that decisions about specific policy issues should be made locally by the agency after consultation with all of the relevant stakeholders.

81. Bureau of Justice Assistance, "Checklist."

82. Body-Worn Camera: Training and Technical Assistance, "Guide for Purchasing."

83. Bureau of Justice Assistance, "Checklist."

84. Sarasota Police Department, "Body Camera Media Day."

85. Bureau of Justice Assistance, "Checklist."

86. Body-Worn Camera: Training and Technical Assistance, "Body-Worn Camera Training."

87. Sherman et al., *Preventing Crime.*

88. Simon, "Sacramento Police Issue New Rules."

89. One of the authors of this book led the study. White, Todak, and Gaub, "Integration and Acceptance."

90. The researchers observed the planning process, start to finish.

91. White, Todak, and Gaub, "Integration and Acceptance," 672.

92. Alpert and McLean, "Where Is the Goal Line?," 685.

93. Ibid.

94. Grubler, "Time for a Change."

95. Klinger, "Spreading Diffusion."

96. White, "Restraint and Technology."

97. Reaves, *Local Police Departments, 2013.*

98. Elinson, "Police Body Camera Footage."

99. Rodriguez, "Immigrant's Shooting at Border."

100. Ikonomova, "Detroit Police Chief Reacts."

101. May, "Woman Said.

102. Ratcliffe, *Reducing Crime.*

103. Tyler and Huo, *Trust in the Law.*

104. Tyler, *Why People Obey the Law*; Tyler and Fagan, "Legitimacy and Cooperation"; Tyler and Huo, *Trust in the Law.*

105. National Institute of Justice, "Law Enforcement"; Center for Evidence-Based Crime Policy, "Evidence-Based Policing Matrix"; United Kingdom College of Policing, "Welcome."

106. Police Executive Research Forum, home page; National Police Foundation, home page; American Society of Evidence-Based Policing, home page; Society of Evidence-Based Policing, home page.
107. Maskaly et al., "Effects of Body-Worn Cameras"; Malm, "Promise of Police Body-Worn Cameras."
108. Lum et al., "Research on Body-Worn Cameras," 115.
109. Law Enforcement Misconduct Statute, 42 U.S.C. § 14141.
110. Guyot, "Bending Granite."

BIBLIOGRAPHY

ACLU New Jersey. "ACLU-NJ Launches Mobile Justice Smartphone App." November 13, 2015. www.aclu-nj.org.

Alpert, Geoffrey P., Dennis Jay Kenney, and Roger Dunham. "Police Pursuits and the Use of Force: Recognizing and Managing 'The Pucker Factor'—A Research Note." *Justice Quarterly* 14, no. 2 (1997): 371–85.

Alpert, Geoffrey P., and Kyle McLean. "Where Is the Goal Line? A Critical Look at Police Body-Worn Camera Programs." *Criminology and Public Policy* 17, no. 3 (2018): 679–88.

American Society of Evidence-Based Policing. Home page. Accessed October 4, 2018. www.americansebp.org.

Anthony, Sebastian. "New Holster Forces All Nearby Body Cams to Start Recording When Gun Is Pulled." *Ars Technica*, February 28, 2017. https://arstechnica.com.

Ariel, Barak. "Police Body Cameras in Large Police Departments." *Journal of Criminal Law and Criminology* 106 (2016).

Ariel, Barak, William A. Farrar, and Ariel Sutherland. "The Effect of Police Body-Worn Cameras on Use of Force and Citizens' Complaints against the Police: A Randomized Controlled Trial." *Journal of Quantitative Criminology* 31, no. 3 (2015): 509–35.

Ariel, Barak, Alex Sutherland, Darren Henstock, Josh Young, Paul Drover, Jayne Sykes, Simon Megicks, and Ryan Henderson. "'Contagious Accountability': A Global Multisite Randomized Controlled Trial on the Effect of Police Body-Worn Cameras on Citizen Complaints against the Police." *Criminal Justice and Behavior* 44, no. 2 (2016): 293–316.

———. "Paradoxical Effects of Self-Awareness of Being Observed: Testing the Effect of Police Body-Worn Cameras on Assaults and Aggression against Officers." *Journal of Experimental Criminology* 14, no. 1 (2018): 19–47.

———. "Report: Increases in Police Use of Force in the Presence of Body-Worn Cameras Are Driven by Officer Discretion: A Protocol-Based Subgroup Analysis of Ten Randomized Experiments." *Journal of Experimental Criminology* 12, no. 3 (2016): 453–63.

———. "Wearing Body Cameras Increases Assaults against Officers and Does Not Reduce Police Use of Force: Results from a Global Multi-Site Experiment." *European Journal of Criminology* 13, no. 6 (2016): 744–55.

Ariel, Barak, Alex Sutherland, and Lawrence W. Sherman. "Preventing Treatment Spillover Contamination in Criminological Field Experiments: The Case for

Body-Worn Police Cameras." *Journal of Experimental Criminology*, 2019. https:// doi.org/10.1007/s11292-018-9344-4.

Arizona Association of Chiefs of Police. "AACOP Sponsors." Accessed October 4, 2018. www.azchiefsofpolice.org.

Associated Press. "LAPD Release First Body Cam Footage after In-Custody Death." *Mercury News* (San Jose, CA), June 20, 2018. www.mercurynews.com.

ASU Center for Violence Prevention and Community Safety, Arizona State University. "Training and Technical Assistance for the U.S. Department of Justice Body-Worn Camera Policy and Implementation Program." Accessed August 31, 2018. http:// cvpcs.asu.edu.

Axon. Home page. Accessed October 4, 2018. www.axon.com.

Berman, Mark. "After Justine Damond Shooting, Minneapolis Police Now Must Turn on Body Cameras for All Calls." *Washington Post*, July 26, 2017.

———. "What the Minneapolis Police Shooting Tells Us about the Limits of Body Cameras." *Washington Post*, July 19, 2017.

Binker, Mark. "New NC Body Camera Law Will Mean Court Order Required for Police Video Release." *WRAL* (Raleigh, NC), September 22, 2016. www.wral.com.

Bobb, Merrick. *13th Semiannual Report*. Los Angeles: Police Assessment Resource Center, 2002.

Body-Worn Camera: Training and Technical Assistance. "About Us." Accessed August 31, 2018. www.bwctta.com.

———. "Body-Worn Camera Policy Review Scorecard." Accessed August 31, 2018. www.bwctta.com.

———. "Body-Worn Camera Resources." Accessed August 31, 2018. www.bwctta.com.

———. "Body Worn Cameras: What You Need to Know." Accessed August 31, 2018. www.bwctta.com.

———. "Body-Worn Camera Training." Accessed August 31, 2018. www.bwctta.com.

———. "A Guide for Purchasing Body-Worn Cameras for State and Local Agencies." Accessed August 31, 2018. http://bwctta.com.

Boivin, Remi, Annie Gendron, Camille Faubert, and Bruno Poulin. "The Body-Worn Camera Perspective Bias." *Journal of Experimental Criminology* 13, no. 1 (2017): 125–42.

Bowman, L. "Tampa Drops Face-Recognition System." *CNET*, August 21, 2003. www .cnet.com.

Braga, Anthony A., James R. Coldren, William Sousa, Denise Rodriguez, D., and Omer Alper. *The Benefits of Body-Worn Cameras: New Findings from a Randomized Controlled Trial at the Las Vegas Metropolitan Police Department*. NCJ-251416. Washington, DC: National Institute of Justice, September 2017.

Braga, Anthony A., William Sousa, James R. Coldren, and Denise Rodriguez. "The Effects of Body-Worn Cameras on Police Activity and Police-Citizen Encounters: A Randomized Controlled Trial." *Journal of Criminal Law and Criminology* 108, no. 3 (2018): 511–38.

Briscoe, Tony. "Judge Says CPD Violated State Labor Laws in Body Cam Expansion." *Chicago Tribune*, January 4, 2018. www.chicagotribune.com.

Bureau of Justice Assistance. "Body-Worn Cameras (BWCS)." Accessed August 31, 2018. www.bja.gov.

——. "Body-Worn Camera Toolkit." Accessed August 31, 2018. www.bja.gov/bwc.

——. "Fraternal Order of Police Body-Worn Cameras ("BWC") Recommended Best Practices." Accessed September 19, 2017. www.bja.gov.

——. "Law Enforcement Implementation Checklist." Accessed August 31, 2018. www .bja.gov.

CALEA. "Law Enforcement Accreditation." Accessed August 31, 2018. www.calea .org.

California Commission on Peace Officer Standards and Training. "POST Monthly Report." Accessed September 5, 2018. http://post.ca.gov.

——. *POST Monthly Report: Keeping You Up to Date on POST Projects (May 2018)*, May 2018. http://post.ca.gov.

Center for Evidence-Based Crime Policy. "Evidence-Based Policing Matrix." Accessed September 19, 2017. http://cebcp.org.

Center for Problem-Oriented Policing, Arizona State University. "26th Annual Problem-Oriented Policing Conference." Accessed October 3, 2018. http://popcen ter.asu.edu.

Chin-Quee, Conrad, J. "The Effects of a Police Body-Worn Camera on Use of Force, Citizen Complaints, and Police Productivity Performance." PhD diss., St. Thomas University, 2018.

Cissner, Amanda B., and Donald J. Farole. *Avoiding Failures of Implementation: Lessons from Process Evaluations*. New York: Center for Court Innovations, 2009.

CNA: Analysis & Solutions. "Safety and Security." Accessed Aug 31, 2018. https://www .cna.org.

Comey, James B. "Law Enforcement and the Communities We Serve: Bending the Lines toward Safety and Justice." Lecture at the University of Chicago Law School, Chicago, IL, October 23, 2015.

COPS (Community Oriented Policing Services), US Department of Justice. "Collaborative Reform Initiative Technical Assistance Center." Accessed September 5, 2018. https://cops.usdoj.gov.

Crow, Matthew S., Jamie A. Snyder, Vaughn J. Crichlow, and John Ortiz Smykla. "Community Perceptions of Police Body-Worn Cameras: The Impact of Views on Fairness, Fear, Performance, and Privacy." *Criminal Justice and Behavior* 44, no. 4 (2017): 589–610.

Culhane, Scott E., John H. Boman IV, and Kimberly Schweitzer. "Public Perceptions of the Justifiability of Police Shootings: The Role of Body-Worn Cameras in a Pre- and Post-Ferguson Experiment." *Police Quarterly* 19, no. 3 (2016): 251–74.

Dann, Carrie, and Andrew Rafferty. "Obama Requests $263 Million for Police Body Cameras, Training." *NBC News*, December 1, 2014. www.nbcnews.com.

Del Pozo, Brandon. "Body Cameras and Privacy—Where Do You Draw the Line?" Police Foundation, 2018. www.policefoundation.org.

de Vries, Reinout E., and Jean-Louis van Gelder. "Explaining Workplace Delinquency: The Role of Honesty-Humility, Ethical Culture, and Employee Surveillance." *Personality and Individual Differences* 86 (2015): 112–16.

Diaz-Zuniga, Lauren. "New Bodycams Start Recording with the Draw of a Gun." *CNN*, July 21, 2017. www.cnn.com.

Dulaney, Josh. "Rialto Police Sex Scandal Investigation Complete." *Daily Breeze* (Torrance, CA), September 9, 2010. www.dailybreeze.com.

Dunn, Chris, and Donna Lieberman. "Body Cameras Are Key for Police Accountability. We Can't Let Them Erode Our Rights." *Washington Post*, June 1, 2017. www.washingtonpost.com.

Edmonton Police Service. *Body Worn Video: Considering the Evidence—Final Report of the Edmonton Police Service Body Worn Video Pilot Project*. Edmonton, AB: Edmonton Police Service, 2015.

Eith, Christine, and Matthew R. Durose. *Contacts between Police and the Public, 2008*. NCJ 234599. United States Bureau of Justice Statistics. Washington, DC: US Government Printing Office, 2011.

Elinson, Zusha. "Police Body Camera Footage Shows Response to Las Vegas Shooting." *Wall Street Journal*, July 3, 2018. www.wsj.com.

Ellis, Tom, Craig Jenkins, and Paul Smith. *Evaluation of the Introduction of Personal Issue Body Worn Video Cameras (Operation Hyperion) on the Isle of Wight: Final Report to Hampshire Constabulary*. Portsmouth, UK: Institute of Criminal Justice Studies, University of Portsmouth, 2015.

Erpenbach, Mary. "The Whole World Is Watching: Camera Phones Put Law Enforcement under Surveillance." *Law Enforcement Technology* 36, no. 2 (2008): 40–41.

Farrar, Tony. *Self-Awareness to Being Watched and Socially Desirable Behavior: A Field Experiment on the Effect of Body-Worn Cameras and Police Use of Force*. Washington, DC: Police Foundation, 2013.

Fjardo, Cristy. "LAPD Body Cam Footage to be Released Within 45 Days under New Proposed Rules." *KCAL9 News* (Los Angeles, CA), February 16, 2018.

Flight, Sander. "Opening Up the Black Box: Understanding the Impact of Bodycams on Policing." *European Police Science and Research Bulletin*, no. 4 (October 2018). https://bulletin.cepol.europa.eu.

Floyd v. City of New York, 959 F. Supp. 2d 540 (S.D.N.Y. 2013).

Fraternal Order of Police. Home page. Accessed September 19, 2017. www.fop.net.

Fyfe, James. "Police Use of Deadly Force: Research and Reform." *Justice Quarterly* 5, no. 2 (1988): 165–205.

Gaub, Janne E., David E. Choate, Natalie Todak, Charles M. Katz, and Michael D. White. "Officer Perceptions of Body-Worn Cameras before and after Deployment: A Study of Three Departments." *Police Quarterly* 19, no. 3 (2016): 275–302.

Gaub, Janne E., Natalie Todak, and Michael D. White. "One Size Doesn't Fit All: The Deployment of Police Body-Worn Cameras to Specialty Units." *International Criminal Justice Review*, July 24, 2018. DOI: 10.1177/1057567718789237.

Gaub, Janne E., Michael D. White, Kathleen E. Padilla, and Charles M. Katz. *Implementing a Police Body-Worn Camera Program in a Small Agency*. Phoenix: Center for Violence Prevention and Community Safety, Arizona State University, 2017.

GbMb. "PB to TB Conversion." Accessed August 31, 2017. www.gbmb.org.

Gershgorn, Dave. "America's Biggest Body-Camera Company Says Facial Recognition Isn't Accurate Enough for Policing Decisions." *Quartz*, August 8, 2018. https://qz.com.

Gillet, Nicolas, Isabelle Huart, Philippe Colombat, and Evelyne Fouquereau. "Perceived Organizational Support, Motivation, and Engagement among Police Officers." *Professional Psychology: Research and Practice* 44 (2013): 46–55.

Goldstein, Herman. "Improving Policing: A Problem-Oriented Approach." *Crime & Delinquency* 25, no. 2 (1979): 236–58.

Goodall, Martin. *Guidance for the Police Use of Body-Worn Video Devices*. London: Home Office, 2007. http://library.college.police.uk.

Goodison, Sean, and Tom Wilson. *Citizen Perceptions of Body-Worn Cameras: A Randomized Controlled Trial*. Washington, DC: Police Executive Research Forum, 2017. https://perf.memberclicks.net.

Grossmith, Lynne, Catherine Owens, Will Finn, David Mann, Tom Davies, and Laura Baika. *Police, Camera, Evidence: London's Cluster Randomised Controlled Trial of Body Worn Video*. London: College of Policing and Mayor's Office for Policing and Crime, 2015.

Grubler, Arnulf. "Time for a Change: On the Patterns of Diffusion of Innovation." *Daedalus* 125, no. 3 (1996): 19–42.

Guyot, Dorothy. "Bending Granite—Attempts to Change the Rank Structure of American Police Departments." *Journal of Police Science and Administration* 7, no 3 (1979): 253–84.

Hamilton, Colby. "Police Union Sues over City's Release of Body Camera Footage, Citing Records-Shielding Law." *New York Law Journal*, January 9, 2018. www.law.com.

Hamm, J. A., A. M. D'Annunzio, B. H. Bornstein, L. Hoetger, and M. N. Herian. "Do Body-Worn Cameras Reduce Eyewitness Cooperation with the Police? An Experimental Inquiry." *Journal of Experimental Criminology*, January 1, 2019, 1–17.

Hannaford-Agor, Paula. "Are Body-Worn Cameras the New CSI Effect?" *Court Manager* 30, no. 3 (2015): 72–73.

Harris, David A. "Picture This: Body Worn Video Devices ('Head Cams') as Tools for Ensuring Fourth Amendment Compliance by Police." Legal Studies Research Paper, Working Paper No. 2010-13, University of Pittsburgh School of Law, 2010.

Harwell, Drew. "Facial Recognition May Be Coming to a Police Body Camera near You." *Washington Post*, April 26, 2018. www.washingtonpost.com.

Headley, Andrea M., Rob T. Guerette, and Auzeen Shariati. "A Field Experiment of the Impact of Body-Worn Cameras (BWCs) on Police Officer Behavior and Perceptions." *Journal of Criminal Justice* 53 (2017): 102–9.

Hedberg, Eric C., Charles M. Katz, and David E. Choate. "Body-Worn Cameras and Citizen Interactions with Police Officers: Estimating Plausible Effects Given Varying Compliance Levels." *Justice Quarterly* 34, no. 4 (2017): 627–51.

Henstock, Darren, and Barak Ariel. "Testing the Effects of Police Body-Worn Cameras on Use of Force during Arrests: A Randomised Controlled Trial in a Large British Police Force." *European Journal of Criminology* 14, no. 6 (2017): 720–50.

Hollinshed, Denise. "Ferguson Police Are Using Body Cameras." *St. Louis Post-Dispatch*, August 31, 2014. www.stltoday.com.

Horowitz, Ben. *The Hard Thing about the Hard Thing: Building a Business When There Are No Easy Answers*. New York: Harper Business, 2014.

Hu, Margaret. "Bulk Biometric Metadata Collection." *North Carolina Law Review* 96 (2017): 1425–74.

Hudson, David. "Building Trust between Communities and Local Police." *The White House* (blog), December 1, 2014. https://obamawhitehouse.archives.gov.

Hyland, Shelley S. *Body-Worn Cameras in Law Enforcement Agencies, 2016*. NCJ 251775. United States Bureau of Justice Statistics. Washington, DC: Office of Justice Programs, US Department of Justice, 2018.

Ikem, Chinelo Nkechi, and Matthew Ogbeifun. "Body Cameras Aren't Working. So What's Next?" *Huffington Post*, November 28, 2017. www.huffingtonpost.com.

Ikonomova, Violet. "Detroit Police Chief Reacts to Officer Beating Naked Woman." *Detroit Metro Times*, August 2, 2018. www.metrotimes.com.

Inouye, Shin. "Scorecard of 50 Local Police Body Camera Programs Shows Nationwide Failure to Protect Civil Rights and Privacy." Leadership Conference, August 2, 2016. https://civilrights.org.

International Association of Chiefs of Police. "Body-Worn Cameras: Model Policy." Accessed September 5, 2018. www.theiacp.org.

———. "Deliberations from the IACP National Forum on Body-Worn Cameras and Violence against Women." 2017. www.theiacp.org.

———. *The Impact of Video Evidence on Modern Policing: Research and Best Practices from the IACP Study on In-Car Cameras*. Alexandria, VA: International Association of Chiefs of Police, 2003.

———. "Welcome to IACP 2019." Accessed September 3, 2018. www.theiacpconference.org.

Introna, Lucak, and Helen Nissenbaum. "Facial Recognition Technology: A Survey of Policy and Implementation Issues." Working Paper No. 2010/030, Lancaster University Management School, 2010. http://eprints.lancs.ac.uk.

James, Tom. "Nevada Likely to Become Second State to Require Police Body Cameras." *Reuters*, May 18, 2017. www.reuters.com.

Jennings, Wesley G., Lorie A. Fridell, and Matthew D. Lynch. "Cops and Cameras: Officer Perceptions of the Use of Body-Worn Cameras in Law Enforcement." *Journal of Criminal Justice* 42, no. 6 (2014): 549–56.

Jennings, Wesley G., Lorie A. Fridell, Mathew D. Lynch, Katelyn K. Jetelina, and Jennifer M. Reingle Gonzalez. "A Quasi-Experimental Evaluation of the Effects of Police Body-Worn Cameras (BWCs) on Response-to-Resistance in a Large Metropolitan Police Department." *Deviant Behavior* 38, no. 11 (2017): 1332–39.

Jennings, Wesley G., Matthew D. Lynch, and Lorie A. Fridell. "Evaluating the Impact of Police Officer Body-Worn Cameras (BWCs) on Response-to-Resistance and Serious External Complaints: Evidence from the Orlando Police Department (OPD) Experience Utilizing a Randomized Controlled Experiment." *Journal of Criminal Justice* 43, no 6 (2015): 480–86.

Johnson, Jason. "Judge Dismisses Mobile's Case on Police Cameras." *Lagniappe Weekly* (Mobile, AL), September 6, 2017. http://lagniappemobile.com.

Justice and Security Strategies, Inc. Home page. Accessed August 31, 2018. www.jssinc.org.

Katz, Charles M., David E. Choate, Justin R. Ready, and Lidia Nuño. *Evaluating the Impact of Officer Worn Body Cameras in the Phoenix Police Department*. Phoenix: Center for Violence Prevention and Community Safety, Arizona State University, 2014.

Kawamoto, Dawn. "If Facial Recognition Comes to Body Cameras, How Will Government Respond?" *GT: Government Technology*, May 1, 2018. www.govtech.com.

Klinger, David A. "Spreading Diffusion in Criminology." *Criminology & Public Policy* 2, no. 3 (2003): 461–68.

Knibbs, Kate. "Seattle Police Put Redacted Body Cam Footage on YouTube." *Gizmodo*, March 3, 2015. https://gizmodo.com.

Koen, Marthinus C., James J. Willis, and Stephen D. Mastrofski. "The Effects of Body-Worn Cameras on Police Organisation and Practice: A Theory-Based Analysis." *Policing and Society*, 2018, 1–17.

Koslicki, Wendy M., David A. Makin, and Dale Willits. "When No One Is Watching: Evaluating the Impact of Body-Worn Cameras on Use of Force Incidents." *Policing and Society*, February 5, 2019, 1–14.

KTLA. "Local Police Officers Accused of Having Group Sex Parties While on Duty." *Huffington Post*, August 6, 2010. www.huffingtonpost.com.

Kyle, Michael J., and David R. White. "The Impact of Law Enforcement Officer Perceptions of Organizational Justice on Their Attitudes Regarding Body-Worn Cameras." *Journal of Crime and Justice* 40 (2017): 68–83.

Las Vegas Metropolitan Police Department. "Body Worn Camera Recordings." Accessed August 31, 2018. www.lvmpd.com.

Laur, Darren, Brendon LeBlanc, Trevor Stephen, Peter Lane, and Debra Taylor. *Proof of Concept Study: Body Worn Video and In Vehicle Video*. Victoria, BC: Victoria Police Department, 2010.

Law Enforcement Executive Forum. Home page. Accessed August 31, 2018. http://law -enforcement-executive-forum.scholasticahq.com.

Lawrence, Daniel S., David McClure, Aili Malm, Matthew Lynch, and Nancy Lavigne. "Activation of Body-Worn Cameras: Variation by Officer, Over Time, and by Policing Activity." *Criminal Justice Review*, May 2, 2019.

Leadership Conference. "Letter to Axon AI Ethics Board Regarding Ethical Product Development and Law Enforcement." April 26, 2018. https://civilrights.org.

Levenson, Michael, and Evan Allen. "Boston Police Union Challenges Body Camera Program." *Boston Globe*, August 26, 2016. www.bostonglobe.com.

Lichtblau, Eric. "F.B.I. Director Says 'Viral Video Effect' Blunts Police Work." *New York Times*, May 11, 2016. www.nytimes.com.

Lillis, Ryan, and Nashelly Chavez. "Cops Muted Their Body Cams after Stephon Clark Shooting. Now They Need to Keep Mikes On." *Sacramento Bee*, April 10, 2018. www.sacbee.com.

Lopez, German. "The Failure of Police Body Cameras." *Vox*, July 21, 2017. www.vox .com.

Los Angeles Police Department. "LAPD Rolls Out First Cameras." August 31, 2015. www.lapdonline.org.

Lovett, Ian. "In California, a Champion for Police Cameras." *New York Times*, August 21, 2013. www.nytimes.com.

Lum, Cynthia, Christopher S. Koper, Linda Merola, Amber Scherer, and Amanda Reioux. *Existing and Ongoing Body Worn Camera Research: Knowledge Gaps and Opportunities*. Fairfax, VA: Center for Evidence-Based Crime Policy, George Mason University, 2015.

Lum, Cynthia, Christopher S. Koper, and James Willis. "Understanding the Limits of Technology's Impact on Police Effectiveness." *Police Quarterly* 20, no. 2 (2017): 135–63.

Lum, Cynthia, Megan Stoltz, Christopher S. Koper, and J. Amber Scherer. "Research on Body-Worn Cameras: What We Know, What We Need to Know." *Criminology and Public Policy* 18, no. 1 (2019): 93–118.

Lussenhop, Jessica. "Police Geeks Trying to Win Over Old-School Cops." *BBC News*, June 25, 2018. www.bbc.com.

MacDonald, Heather. *The War on Cops: How the New Attack on Law and Order Makes Everyone Less Safe*. New York: Encounter Books, 2016.

Maguire, Edward R., Justin Nix, and Bradley A. Campbell. "A War on Cops? The Effects of Ferguson on the Number of U.S. Police Officers Murdered in the Line of Duty." *Justice Quarterly* 34, no. 5 (2017): 739–58. https://doi.org/10.1080/07418825.20 16.1236205.

Major Cities Chiefs and Major County Sheriffs Associations. *Survey of Technology Needs: Body Worn Cameras*. Washington, DC: DHS Office of Emergency Communications, 2015.

Major Cities Chiefs Association. "Conference Overview." Accessed August 31, 2018. http://mcca.wildapricot.org.

Malm, Aili. "The Promise of Police Body-Worn Cameras." *Criminology and Public Policy* 18, no. 1 (2019).

Manning, Peter K. "The Police Mandate: Strategies and Appearances." In *Policing: A View from the Street*, edited by Peter K. Manning and John Van Maanen, 7–31. Santa Monica, CA: Goodyear, 1978.

———. *The Technology of Policing*. New York: NYU Press, 2008.

Marlow, Chad, and Jay Stanley. "We're Updating Our Police Body Camera Recommendations for Even Better Accountability and Civil Liberties Protections." ACLU, January 25, 2018. www.aclu.org.

Martin, Angela J., Jackie M. Wellen, and Martin R. Grimmer. "An Eye on Your Work: How Empowerment Affects the Relationship between Electronic Surveillance and Counterproductive Work Behaviours." *International Journal of Human Resource Management* 27, no. 21 (2016): 2635–51.

Maskaly, John, Christopher Donner, Wesley G. Jennings, Barak Ariel, and Alex Sutherland. "The Effects of Body-Worn Cameras (BWCs) on Police and Citizen Outcomes: A State-of-the-Art Review." *Policing: An International Journal of Police Strategies and Management* 40 (2017): 672–88.

May, Ashley. "A Woman Said a Texas State Trooper Sexually Assaulted Her. Her Lawyer Apologized after Seeing Body Cam Video." *USA Today*, May 23, 2018. www.usatoday.com.

Mazerolle, Lorraine, Emma Antrobus, Sarah Bennett, and Tom R. Tyler. "Shaping Citizen Perceptions of Police Legitimacy: A Randomized Field Trial of Procedural Justice." *Criminology* 51, no. 1 (2013): 33–63.

McCale, Christina. "Research and Policy Issues Use of Body-Worn Cameras: An Interview with Dr. Michael White." *Justice Clearinghouse*, July 17, 2018. https://justiceclearinghouse.com.

McClure, Dave, Nancy La Vigne, Mathew Lynch, Laura Golian, Daniel Lawrence, and Aili Malm. *How Body Cameras Affect Community Members' Perceptions of Police: Results from a Randomized Controlled Trial of One Agency's Pilot*. Washington, DC: Urban Institute, 2017.

McCluskey, John D., Craig D. Uchida, Shellie E. Solomon, Alese Wooditch, Christine Connor, and Lauren Revier. "Assessing the Effects of Body-Worn Cameras on Procedural Justice in the Los Angeles Police Department." *Criminology* 57, no. 2 (2019): 208–36.

Meadows, Jonah. "Evanston Police Want to Expand Bodycam to All Sworn Officers." *Evanston (IL) Patch*, July 23, 2018.

Merola, Linda, Cynthia Lum, Christopher S. Koper, and Amber Scherer. *Body Worn Cameras and the Courts: A National Survey of State Prosecutors*. Fairfax, VA: Center for Evidence-Based Crime Policy, George Mason University, 2016.

Mesa Police Department. *On-Officer Body Camera System: Program Evaluation and Recommendations*. Mesa, AZ: Mesa Police Department, 2015.

Metz, Cade, and Natasha Singer. "Newspaper Shooting Shows Widening Use of Facial Recognition by Authorities." *New York Times*, June 29, 2018. www.nytimes.com.

Miller, J. Mitchell, and Holly Ventura Miller. "Rethinking Program Fidelity for Criminal Justice." *Criminology & Public Policy* 14, no. 2 (2015): 339–49.

Miller, Lindsay, Jessica Toliver, and Police Executive Research Forum. *Implementing a Body-Worn Camera Program: Recommendations and Lessons Learned*. Washington, DC: Office of Community Oriented Policing Services, 2014.

Mitchell, Nicholas E. *2014 Annual Report*. Denver, CO: Office of the Independent Monitor, 2015.

Mitchell, Renée J., Barak Ariel, Maria Emilia Firpo, Ricardo Fraiman, Federico del Castillo, Jordan M. Hyatt, Cristobal Weinborn, and Hagit Brants Sabo. "Measuring the Effect of Body-Worn Cameras on Complaints in Latin America: The Case of Traffic Police in Uruguay." *Policing: An International Journal* 41, no. 4 (2018): 510–24.

Morgan, Stephen L., and Joel A. Pally. *Ferguson, Gray, and Davis: An Analysis of Recorded Crime Incidents and Arrests in Baltimore City, March 2010 through December 2015*. Baltimore: Johns Hopkins University, 21st Century Cities Initiative, 2016. http://socweb.soc.jhu.edu.

Morrow, Weston J., Charles M. Katz, and David E. Choate. "Assessing the Impact of Police Body-Worn Cameras on Arresting, Prosecuting, and Convicting Suspects of Intimate Partner Violence." *Police Quarterly* 19, no. 3 (2016): 303–25.

Motorola Solutions. "Police Body Cameras and In-Car Cameras." Accessed August 31, 2018. www.motorolasolutions.com.

Munger, Kristen, and Shelby J. Harris. "Effects of an Observer on Handwashing in a Public Restroom." *Perceptual and Motor Skills* 69, no 3 (1989): 733–34.

Murphy, Shelley, and Haiwatha Bray. "Face Recognition Devices Failed in Test at Logan." *Boston Globe*, September 3, 2003. http://archive.boston.com.

National Institute of Justice. "Law Enforcement." Accessed September 4, 2018. www.crimesolutions.gov.

———. "Sentinel Events Initiative." November 1, 2017.

National Police Foundation. Home page. Accessed September 4, 2018. www.policefoundation.org.

Newman, Lily Hay. "Police Bodycams Can Be Hacked to Doctor Footage." *Wired*, August 11, 2018. https://www.wired.com.

Nix, Justin, and Scott E. Wolfe. "Sensitivity to the Ferguson Effect: The Role of Managerial Organizational Justice." *Journal of Criminal Justice* 47 (2016): 12–20.

Nored, Lisa S., Philip E. Carlan, and Doug Goodman. "Incentives and Obstacles to Drug Court Implementation: Observations of Drug Court Judges and Administrators." *Justice Policy Journal* 6, no. 1 (2009).

Nowacki, Jeffrey S., and Dale Willits. "Adoption of Body Cameras by United States Police Agencies: An Organisational Analysis." *Policing and Society* 28, no. 7 (2018): 841–53.

ODS Consulting. *Body Worn Video Projects in Paisley and Aberdeen, Self-Evaluation.* Glasgow, UK: ODS Consulting, 2011.

Ohlin, Lloyd E. "The President's Commission on Law Enforcement and Administration of Justice." In *Sociology and Public Policy: The Case of Presidential Commissions,* edited by Mirra Komarovsky, 93–115. New York: Elsevier, 1975.

Owens, Catherine, David Mann, and Rory McKenna. *The Essex Body Worn Video Trial: The Impact of Body Worn Video on Criminal Justice Outcomes of Domestic Abuse Incidents.* London: College of Policing, 2014.

Pegues, Jeff. "Law Enforcement Increasing Use of Facial Recognition Technology." *CBS News,* October 18, 2016. www.cbsnews.com.

Pelfrey, William V., Jr., and Steven Keener. "Police Body Worn Cameras: A Mixed Method Approach Assessing Perceptions of Efficacy." *Policing: An International Journal of Police Strategies & Management* 39, no. 3 (2016): 491–506. https://doi .org/10.1108/PIJPSM-02-2016-0019.

Peterson, Bryce E., Lilly Yu, Nancy La Vigne, and Daniel S. Lawrence. *The Milwaukee Police Department's Body-Worn Camera Program: Evaluation Findings and Key Takeaways.* Washington, DC: Urban Institute, 2018.

Pew Charitable Trusts. "Implementation Oversight for Evidence-Based Programs: A Policymaker's Guide to Effective Program Delivery." May 3, 2016. www.pewtrusts.org.

Phelps, Joshua M., Jon Strype, Sophie Le Bellu, Saadi Lahlou, and Jan Aandal. "Experiential Learning and Simulation Based Training in Norwegian Police Education: Examining Body-Worn Video as a Tool to Encourage Reflection." *Policing: A Journal of Police and Practice* 12, no. 1 (2016): 50–65.

Phillips, Scott W. "Eyes Are Not Cameras: The Importance of Integrating Perceptual Distortions, Misinformation, and False Memories into the Police Body Camera Debate." *Policing: A Journal of Policy and Practice* 12, no. 1 (2016): 91–99.

Pilant, Lois. "Spotlight on In-Car Video Systems." *Police Chief* 62, no. 4 (1995): 30–31, 33–37.

"Police Body Cameras: Money for Nothing?" *Fox News,* October 20, 2017. www .foxnews.com.

Police Executive Research Forum. *Costs and Benefits of Body-Worn Camera Deployments.* Washington, DC: Office of Community Oriented Policing Services, 2018.

———. Home page. Accessed September 5, 2018. www.policeforum.org.

Police Foundation. "Body-Worn Camera Study by Executive Fellow Chief Tony Farrar Is Published in Scientific Journal." Accessed September 5, 2018. www.policefounda tion.org.

PoliceOne. Home page. Accessed October 1, 2018. www.policeone.com.

Police Policy Studies Council. Home page. Accessed October 4, 2018. www.theppsc .org.

President's Commission on Law Enforcement and Administration of Justice. *Task Force Report: The Courts*. Washington, DC: US Government Printing Office, 1967.

President's Task Force on 21st Century Policing. *Final Report of the President's Task Force on 21st Century Policing*. Washington, DC: Office of Community Oriented Policing Services, 2015.

Pretrial Justice Institute. "Pretrial Services Program Implementation: A Starter Kit." Washington, DC: Bureau of Justice Assistance, 2009. www.ncjrs.gov.

Pyrooz, David C., Scott H. Decker, Scott E. Wolfe, and John A. Shjarback "Was There a Ferguson Effect on Crime Rates in Large U.S. Cities?" *Journal of Criminal Justice* 46 (2016): 1–8. https://doi.org/10.1016/j.jcrimjus.2016.01.001.

Ratcliffe, Jerry H. *Reducing Crime: A Companion for Police Leaders*. New York: Routledge, 2018.

———. *Video Surveillance of Public Places*. Problem-Oriented Guides for Police: Response Guides Series. Washington: DC: Center for Problem-Oriented Policing, 2011.

Ready, Justin T., and Jacob T. N. Young. "The Impact of On-Officer Video Cameras on Police-Citizen Contacts: Findings from a Controlled Experiment in Mesa, AZ." *Journal of Experimental Criminology* 11, no. 3 (2015): 445–58.

Reaves, Brian A. *Local Police Departments, 2013: Equipment and Technology*. NCJ 248767. United States Bureau of Justice Statistics. Washington, DC: Office of Justice Programs, 2015.

Reno, Janet, Raymond C. Fisher, Laurie Robinson, and Nancy E. Gist. *Critical Elements in the Planning, Development, and Implementation of Successful Correctional Options*. NCJ 168966. United States Bureau of Justice Statistics. Washington, DC: Office of Justice Programs, 1998.

Reuland, Melissa Miller. *A Guide to Implementing Police-Based Diversion Programs for People with Mental Illness*. Delmar, NY: Technical Assistance and Policy Analysis Center for Jail Diversion, 2014.

Reuters. "Obama Calls for Body Cameras on Police." *New York Times*, December 2, 2014. www.nytimes.com.

Ripley, Amanda. "A Big Test of Police Body Cameras Defies Expectations." *New York Times*, October 20, 2017. www.nytimes.com.

Ripley, Amanda, and Timothy Williams. "Body Cameras Have Little Effect on Police Behavior, Study Says." *New York Times*, October 20, 2017. www.nytimes.com.

Rodriguez, Jesus. "Immigrant's Shooting at Border Fuels Push for Body Cameras." *Politico*, June 11, 2018. www.politico.com.

Rogers, Everett M. *Diffusion of Innovations*. New York: Free Press, 1995.

Roy, Allyson. "On-Officer Video Cameras: Examining the Effects of Police Department Policy and Assignment on Camera Use and Activation." Master's thesis, Arizona State University, Phoenix, 2014.

Rushin, Stephen, and Griffin Edwards. "De-policing." *Cornell Law Review* 102 (2017).

Ryan, Bryce, and Neal C. Gross. "The Diffusion of Hybrid Seed Corn in Two Iowa Communities." *Rural Sociology* 8 (1943): 15–24.

Sadd, Susan, and Randolph M. Grinc. *Policing: Innovative Neighborhood-Oriented Policing in Eight Cities.* Washington, DC: National Institute of Justice, 1994.

Sagan, Carl. *Billions and Billions: Thoughts on Life and Death at the Brink of the Millennium.* London: Headline, 1999.

Sarasota Police Department. "Sarasota Police Department Body Camera Media Day." YouTube, February 25, 2015. https://www.youtube.com/watch?v=s27Rmf SQSYM.

Seattle Police Department. "1.115—Media Release: Officer-Involved Shooting." Last updated June 1, 2017. www.seattle.gov.

Shelton, Donald E. "The 'CSI Effect': Does It Really Exist?" *National Institute of Justice Journal* 259 (2008).

Sherman, Lawrence W., Denise C. Gottfredson, Doris L. MacKenzie, John Eck, Peter Reuter, and Shawn D. Bushway. *Preventing Crime: What Works, What Doesn't, What's Promising.* NCJ-171676. National Institute of Justice. Washington, DC: US Government Printing Office, 1998.

Shjarback, John A., David C. Pyrooz, Scott E. Wolfe, and Scott H. Decker. "De-policing and Crime in the Wake of Ferguson: Racialized Changes in the Quantity and Quality of Policing among Missouri Police Departments." *Journal of Criminal Justice* 50 (2017): 42–52. https://doi.org/10.1016/j.jcrimjus.2017.04.003.

Simon, Darran. "Sacramento Police Issue New Rules on Muting Body Cameras." *CNN*, April 11, 2018.

Singer, Natasha. "Amazon's Facial Recognition Wrongly Identifies 28 Lawmakers, A.C.L.U. Says." *New York Times*, July 26, 2018. www.nytimes.com.

Society of Evidence-Based Policing. Home page. Accessed August 31, 2018. www.sebp .police.uk.

Sousa, William H., Terance D. Miethe, and Mari Sakiyama. "Inconsistencies in Public Opinion of Body-Worn Cameras on Police: Transparency, Trust, and Improved Police-Citizen Relationships." *Policing: A Journal of Policy and Practice* 12, no 1 (2017): 100–108.

Stanley, Jay. *Police Body-Mounted Cameras: With Right Policies in Place, a Win for All.* New York: American Civil Liberties Union, 2015.

Stoltzenberg, Lisa, Stewart J. D'Allessio, and Jamie L. Flexon. *Eyes on the Street: Police Use of Body-Worn Cameras in Miami-Dade County.* Weston, FL: Weston, 2019.

Stoughton, Seth W. "Police Body-Worn Cameras." *North Carolina Law Review* 96, no 5 (2018): 1363–1424.

Sunshine, Jason, and Tom R. Tyler. "The Role of Procedural Justice and Legitimacy in Shaping Public Support for Policing." *Law & Society Review* 37 (2003): 513–48.

Sutherland, Alex, Barak Ariel, William Farrar, and Randy De Anda. "Post-Experimental Follow-Ups—Fade-Out versus Persistence Effects: The Rialto Police Body-Worn Camera Experiment Four Years On." *Journal of Criminal Justice* 53 (2017): 110–16.

Swire, Peter, and Jesse Woo. "Privacy and Cybersecurity Lessons at the Intersection of the Internet of Things and Police Body-Worn Cameras." *North Carolina Law Review* 96 (2017): 1475–1523.

Taylor, Emmeline, Murray Lee, Matthew Willis, and Alexandra Gannoni. "Police Detainee Perspectives on Police Body-Worn Cameras." *Trends & Issues in Crime and Criminal Justice* 537 (2017).

Terrill, William, and Eugene A. Paoline III. "Police Use of Less Lethal Force: Does Administrative Policy Matter?" *Justice Quarterly* 34, no. 2 (2017): 193–216.

Todak, Natalie, Janne E. Gaub, and Michael D. White. "The Importance of External Stakeholders for Police Body-Worn Camera Diffusion." *Policing: An International Journal of Police Strategies & Management* 41, no. 4 (2018): 448–64.

Toronto Police Service. *Body-Worn Cameras: A Report on the Findings of the Pilot Project to Test the Value and Feasibility of Body-Worn Cameras for Police Officers in Toronto.* Toronto, ON: Toronto Police Department Strategy Management—Strategic Planning Team, June 2016.

Tyler, Tom R. "Psychological Perspectives on Legitimacy and Legitimation." *Annual Review of Psychology* 57 (2006): 375–400.

———. *Why People Obey the Law.* New Haven, CT: Yale University Press, 1990.

Tyler, Tom R., and Jeffrey Fagan. "Legitimacy and Cooperation: Why Do People Help the Police Fight Crime in Their Communities?" *Ohio State Journal of Criminal Law* 6 (2008): 231.

Tyler, Tom R., Phillip Atiba Goff, and Robert J. MacCoun. "The Impact of Psychological Science on Policing in the United States: Procedural Justice, Legitimacy, and Effective Law Enforcement." *Psychological Science in the Public Interest* 16, no. 3 (2015): 75–109.

Tyler, Tom R., and Yuen Huo. *Trust in the Law: Encouraging Public Cooperation with the Police and Courts.* New York: Russell Sage Foundation, 2002.

Tyler, Tom R., and Cheryl J. Wakslak. "Profiling and Police Legitimacy: Procedural Justice, Attributions of Motive, and Acceptance of Police Authority." *Criminology* 42, no. 2 (2004): 253–82.

United Kingdom College of Policing. "Welcome to the Crime Reduction Toolkit." Accessed October 4, 2018. http://whatworks.college.police.uk.

———. "What Is Evidence-Based Policing?" Accessed August 31, 2018. http://what works.college.police.uk.

United States Bureau of Justice Statistics. "Data Collection: Law Enforcement Management and Administrative Statistics (LEMAS)." Accessed September 3, 2018. www.bjs.gov.

Urban Institute. "Police Body-Worn Camera Legislation Tracker." Last updated October 29, 2018. http://apps.urban.org.

Van Rompay, Thomas J., Dorette J. Vonk, and Marieke L. Fransen. "The Eye of the Camera: Effects of Security Cameras on Prosocial Behavior." *Environment and Behavior* 41, no. 1 (2009): 60–74.

VIEVU. Home page. Accessed October 4, 2018. www.vievu.com.

Wahl, Georgia M., Bridget Gardner, Alan B. Marr, John P. Hunt, Norman E. McSwain, Christopher C. Baker, and Juan Duchesne. "Red Light Cameras: Do They Change Driver Behavior and Reduce Accidents?" *Journal of Trauma and Acute Care Surgery* 68, no. 3 (2010): 515–18.

Walker, Samuel. "Police Accountability: Current Issues and Research Needs." In *National Institute of Justice (NIJ) Policing Research Workshop: Planning for the Future*. Washington, DC: US Government Printing Office, 2006.

Walker, Samuel, and Carol A. Archbold. *The New World of Police Accountability*. Thousand Oaks, CA: Sage, 2014.

Walker, Samuel, and Charles M. Katz. *Police in America: An Introduction*. 8th ed. New York: McGraw-Hill, 2012.

Wallace, Danielle, Michael D. White, Janne E. Gaub, and Natalie Todak. "Body-Worn Cameras as a Potential Source of De-policing: Testing for Camera-Induced Passivity." *Criminology* 56, no. 3 (2018): 481–509.

WatchGuard. Home page. Accessed August 30, 2018. http://watchguardvideo.com.

Weisburd, David, Stephen D. Mastrofski, Ann Marie McNally, Rosann Greenspan, and James J. Willis. "Reforming to Preserve: Compstat and Strategic Problem Solving in American Policing." *Criminology & Public Policy* 2, no. 3 (2003): 421–56.

Wejnert, Barbara. "Integrating Models of Diffusion of Innovations: A Conceptual Framework." *Annual Review of Sociology* 28, no. 1 (2002): 297–326.

Welsh, Brandon C., and David P. Farrington. "Public Area CCTV and Crime Prevention: An Updated Systematic Review and Meta-Analysis." *Justice Quarterly* 26, no. 4 (2009): 716–45. doi:10.1080/07418820802506206.

White, Michael D. "Controlling Police Decisions to Use Deadly Force: Reexamining the Importance of Administrative Policy. *Crime & Delinquency* 47, no. 1 (2001): 131–51.

———. *Current Issues and Controversies in Policing*. Boston: Allyn and Bacon / Pearson, 2007.

———. *Police Officer Body-Worn Cameras: Assessing the Evidence*. Washington, DC: US Department of Justice, Office of Justice Programs, 2014.

———. "Restraint and Technology: Exploring Police Use of the TASER through the Diffusion of Innovation Framework." In *Oxford Handbook on Police and Policing*, edited by Michael D. Reisig and Robert J. Kane, 280–301. New York: Oxford University Press, 2014.

White, Michael D., and James Coldren. "Body-Worn Cameras: Separating Fact from Fiction." *PM Magazine*, February 12, 2017. https://icma.org.

White, Michael D., Michaela Flippin, and Charles M. Katz. *Policy and Practice: A Three-Year Policy Analysis of U.S. Department of Justice-Funded Law Enforcement*

Agencies. Phoenix: Center for Violence Prevention and Community Safety, Arizona State University, 2018.

White, Michael D., and Henry F. Fradella. *Stop and Frisk: The Use and Abuse of a Controversial Policing Tactic*. New York: NYU Press, 2016.

White, Michael D., Janne E. Gaub, Aili Malm, and Kathleen E. Padilla. "Implicate or Exonerate? The Impact of Police Body-Worn Cameras on the Adjudication of Drug and Alcohol Cases." *Policing: A Journal of Policy and Practice*, July 6, 2019. https://doi.org/10.1093/police/paz043.

White, Michael D., Janne E. Gaub, and Kathleen E. Padilla. "Impacts of BWCs on Citizen Complaints: Directory of Outcomes." United States Bureau of Justice Assistance, Body-Worn Camera Training and Technical Assistance. Accessed September 4, 2018. www.bwctta.com.

———. "Impacts of BWCs on Use of Force: Directory of Outcomes." United States Bureau of Justice Assistance, Body-Worn Camera Training and Technical Assistance. Accessed September 4, 2018. www.bwctta.com.

White, Michael D., Janne E. Gaub, and Natalie Todak. "To Record or Not to Record? An Investigation of Body-Worn Camera Activation." Paper presented at the Academy of Criminal Justice Sciences Meeting, New Orleans, LA, February 2018.

White, Michael D., Philip Mulvey, and Lisa Dario. "Arrestees and Their Perceptions of the Police: Exploring Procedural Justice, Legitimacy, and Willingness to Cooperate with Police across Offender Types." *Criminal Justice and Behavior* 43, no. 3 (2016): 343–64.

White, Michael D., Natalie Todak, and Janne E. Gaub. "Assessing Citizen Perceptions of Body-Worn Cameras after Encounters with Police." *Policing: An International Journal of Police Strategies & Management* 40, no. 4 (2017): 689–703.

———. "Examining Body-Worn Camera Integration and Acceptance among Police Officers, Citizens, and External Stakeholders." *Criminology & Public Policy* 17, no. 3 (2018): 649–77.

Williams, Brandt. "Minneapolis Officer Failed to Turn on Body Cameras before Fatal Shooting." *NPR*, July 18, 2017. www.npr.org.

Williams, Clarence, and Justice W. Moyer. "One Month after D.C. Police Shooting, Answers Remain Elusive." *Washington Post*, October 10, 2016. www.washingtonpost.com.

Williams, Timothy, James Thomas, Samuel Jacoby, and Damien Cave. "Police Body Cameras: What Do You See?" *New York Times*, April 1, 2016.

Winton, Richard. "2 Rialto Police Officers Resign, 4 Disciplined amid Sex Scandal Investigation." *Los Angeles Times Blog*, November 19, 2010. http://latimesblogs.latimes.com.

Wolfe, Scott E., and Justice Nix. "Police Officers' Trust in Their Agency: Does Self-Legitimacy Protect against Supervisor Procedural Injustice?" *Criminal Justice and Behavior* 44, no. 5 (2017): 717–32.

Wood, Colin. "Police Could Be Doing So Much More with Body Cameras, Says For-
    mer Chief." *StateScoop*, January 22, 2018. https://statescoop.com.
Woodward, John D., Jr., Christopher Horn, Julius Gatune, and Aryn Thomas. *Biomet-
    rics: A Look at Facial Recognition*. Santa Monica, CA: Rand, 2003.
Yant, Bryan. "Officers Get Raise for Wearing Body Cams." PubSec Alliance, September
    28, 2016. http://lvppa.com.
Yokum, David, Anita Ravishankar, and Alexander Coppock. *Evaluating the Effects of
    Police Body-Worn Cameras: A Randomized Controlled Trial*. Washington, DC: The
    Lab @ DC, Office of the City Administrator, Executive Office of the Mayor, 2017.

INDEX

ABOUT THE AUTHORS

Michael D. White is Professor in the School of Criminology and Criminal Justice at Arizona State University and is Associate Director of ASU's Center for Violence Prevention and Community Safety. He is also Director of the Doctoral Program in Criminology and Criminal Justice at ASU. He received his PhD in criminal justice from Temple University in 1999. Prior to entering academia, he worked as a deputy sheriff in Pennsylvania.

Aili Malm is Professor in the School of Criminology, Criminal Justice, and Emergency Management at California State University, Long Beach. She received her PhD in criminology from Simon Fraser University in 2006.